GHOST
WALTZ

GHOST WALTZ

A MEMOIR BY
INGEBORG DAY

THE VIKING PRESS   NEW YORK

Copyright © Ingeborg Day, 1980
All rights reserved
First published in 1980 by The Viking Press
625 Madison Avenue, New York, N.Y. 10022
Published simultaneously in Canada by
Penguin Books Canada Limited

LIBRARY OF CONGRESS CATALOGING IN PUBLICATION DATA
Day, Ingeborg.
Ghost waltz.
1. Day, Ingeborg. 2. Austria—Biography.
3. United States—Biography. I. Title.
CT918.D39A3   943.6'052   80–16411
ISBN 0–670–29485–3

Printed in the United States of America
Set in Linotron Electra

Grateful acknowledgment is made to the following for per-
mission to reprint copyrighted material:

Atlantis Verlag AG: A selection from *Die Schwierigen oder
J'adore ce qui me brûle* by Max Frisch. English translation by
Ingeborg Day.
Diamond and Wilson: Portions of lyrics from "Heroes" by
David Bowie; music by David Bowie and Brian Eno. © 1977
Bewlay Bros. Music, Fleur Music, Ltd., EG Music Ltd. All
rights reserved.
Elie Wiesel: Quotation from "The Long Search," PBS.

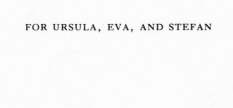

FOR URSULA, EVA, AND STEFAN

We can be Heroes
We can be Heroes
We can be Heroes
Just for one day
We're nothing
And nothing will help us
But we could be safer
Just for one day.

"Heroes," lyrics by David Bowie
music by Bowie-Eno

For I the Lord thy God am a jealous God, visiting the
iniquity of the fathers upon the children unto the third and
fourth generation of them that hate me.

Exodus 20:5

We are one body. He who forgets himself, forgets his son;
he who shuns his father, shuns himself.

Max Frisch,
Die Schwierigen oder J'adore ce qui me brûle

I don't understand the victims, and I don't understand the
killers. But the victims are my problem, and the killers are
yours.

Elie Wiesel, PBS, "The Long Search"

Remember, we're all in this alone.

Lily Tomlin

GHOST
WALTZ

I had two sets of parents. The set I remember adopted me in 1945, when I was four. They loved me and did for me what was within their power under circumstances they taught me to accept as hostile; you worked hard in such a world and you kept to yourself.

Only glimpses remain to me of another couple, thrilling, luxurious. An exuberant man swings me high into the air above him, his upturned face aglow. A succulent, rose-gold woman laughs shimmering cascades as I learn to walk.

My adoptive parents never referred to my real parents. Early on I assumed that what had made necessary this transfer of a child from one sort of family to another was *The War*. Of all explanations and nonexplanations, *The War* was the most unassailable. God was no match for it. When I was nine or ten, my adoptive father sometimes argued with me about the existence of God. Fortified with phrases from my religious education classes, I believed in such an existence. He did not. The argument was meant as—and was—a treat for me. Time simply "spent" with children was rare.

One could discuss God but not *The War*, how it had come about or what, and who, had been involved, though the last of these questions was easy to figure out, even for a child. It had been "us" against, well, the Americans, and, let's see, the Russians, and the French, too, and of course there'd been the English, whose occupation forces were quartered less than a block from where we lived. The most daring of the neighborhood children (ill-concealed behind gray wood posts that held up clotheslines sagging under sheets) would shout to impassive faces: Tommy-go-home.

It was not in my vocabulary to ask my adoptive parents about my real, my former parents. Not once while they were alive was I able to find the words: Look folks, what happened to you? What changed you so?

"Do not exaggerate, the truth suffices." Professor Doctor Szekely once wrote that on a composition of mine. She used the formal *Sie*, the first adult to address me in this manner, I was twelve. Her short, white hair was held behind each ear with a silvery pin, tweed suits accentuated her fragile grace. Her passions were language and the teaching of German, and because I was in love with her I loved the subject she taught and wanted to spend my life writing compositions, which she might grace with profound and oracular comments using *Sie*.

Would she write "do not exaggerate" across my paper now? Of

course I wasn't adopted. Of course the difference wasn't that extreme. Of course my parents laughed after 1945 too, sometimes they told jokes, once my father danced with me. But it's no exaggeration at the crux of it, at the soul of it.

The woman in a flowered dress has already published a book on the topic being explored, and the one in black has nearly finished writing hers. They are talk-show guests, discussing the rewards and perils inherent in being a mistress. I scrutinize the women's mouths and bodies and try to imagine what they do in bed, and whether what they do is more adventurous than what their lovers' wives are accustomed to doing. It is not a rewarding speculation, though it results in the spineless calm that sometimes accompanies doing what is expected of one: in question after question, the host panders to an audience he assumes is thinking what I am thinking. He leers, and winks and leers.

Dialing full circle produces nothing but commercials, I am tired of reading, and it's too early to go to sleep. Through half-closed eyes I watch the women converge on their host and wind microphone cords around his neck, carefully following the line where wavy white hair meets the collar of a made-to-order shirt; he gasps and promises never to sneer in public again. . . . But the mistresses have left, the first part of the program is over, there is more to come.

Seven or eight men are introduced, writers, writer-historians, historians, a psychiatrist. They have gathered to discuss the fascination a man named Adolf Hitler holds for the public, why so many books have been written about him—nearly fifty thousand between 1945 and 1975 alone, claims one of the historians; though his neighbor contests this figure, an amiable consensus continues to prevail—the components of National Socialism, genocide, lunacy and evil, and whether there is a difference between the latter two.

One scholar takes exception, with all due respect, to what another has succeeded in advancing. A third agrees with the former, though in direction only, not in emphasis—or maybe the direction is shaky and the emphasis is richly deserved—while someone in the corner labels the thrust of the current argument not the most productive, and suggests that his colleagues consider instead his very own emphasis and direction. These are men devoted to their specialty, the one who has published most recently looking more genuinely at ease than his peers, the book is doing well. I have stopped switching channels. The host does not condescend to this group, he is impressed and eager to impress in turn. "How did it happen?" he asks. And, gravely, again, "What made it possible for it all to happen?"

There is a hush, then the guests dive into the void at once. Their genial moderator soothes and sorts them into order until they deliver themselves of differing theories one by one. Riveted, I listen to each. On the nearest piece of paper I scribble the answer that resonates most profoundly, the man pronouncing it makes it easy for me; he repeats the phrase twice, slowly and emphatically, his somber face given over to the camera as a sun worshiper's, ". . . the comprehensive crisis of a capitalist economy." While the host says, ". . . short pause," I look down at what turns out to be my grocery list for tomorrow: milk, bologna, peaches, toilet paper—my needs rendered vaguely ominous, titled as they are by the historian's statement. I watch the men lean toward each other in soundless conversation as the camera pulls up and back, then I turn off the set.

Better to speculate about the plight of the kept woman in today's-society-in-transition-blah-blah, I think, even that may come in handy someday. What use, on the other hand, will these learned men's pronouncements be to me, their fascination with a minuscule portion of the topic they have made their life's work? I know better. Hitler got as far as he did for one reason, a simple one. "It all happened" because my father joined his party and idolized him, and because my mother did and felt whatever my father did and felt, and enormous masses of people did and felt as my parents did and felt. And a comprehensive crisis of a capitalist economy it may well have been, and a lot of other things too, but that's neither here nor there for me.

My parents are dead and I need to think highly of them.

By "highly" I mean: I need to think of my parents as an ordinary couple surrounded by ordinary numbers. Two children, forty-two Schillings, three days to Christmas, seventy-eight kilometers to our grandparents' farm. I need to think of my parents as an ordinary couple unconnected to the numbers that in some of my night-mares they expose to me on their bared wrists. (My mother pushes up the sleeve of a sweater she has knitted for herself, my father turns back the frayed cuff of a plaid workshirt, newly washed, ironed with care.) I need to think of my parents as an ordinary couple counting ordinary numbers, unencumbered by tattoos: Six Million. A large six, six perfectly rounded zeros.

A psychiatrist says to me, "What's the matter with you, who do you think you are, anyway! You think those two little people caused it all? What kind of megalomania is that!"

That isn't the point, though. Even if they did not "cause it all," even if they did not cause anything, directly, one prefers not to have one's parents lumped with history's worst: Nazis.

Clearly, that's not the point either. The point is, Six Million is unimaginable. If my parents were connected—at all, any which way—with the amassing of this number, then they are unimaginable too.

My father (the former Nazi, the man I remember) did not speak about Hitler, *The War*, or Jews. I wish I could have known the boy who grew up to be the man who became the Nazi. As it is, most of what I have is conjecture.

I still don't know if my mother belonged to the party, but she loved my father. They happened to sit next to each other in a movie theater in 1937 and toward the end of the show she cried and he offered her a handkerchief and she adored him from then on and never slept with another man.

If I think Six Million, my parents become monstrous in my brain and more monstrous and then so monstrous that I fight for breath and they become abstract. Abstract, they are specimens to me, and I begin to breathe again. I cannot think, Six Million, and see my parents (*Mutti, Vati*) in personal terms. In order to envision my parents, I have become adept at scores of highly specific, varying maneuvers of my own design. These maneuvers are as convoluted, intricate, eerie, and without apparent pattern as certain works of lace, madness-made-decorative, fashioned by inmates of a Belgian insane asylum. "Marvels," one art critic dubbed them. As I spin out my maneuvers, I conjure up anonymous, mad lacemakers (silently moving their lips, frowning in concentration) laboring at theirs. Mine do not result in a visible product. They consist of relentless attempts—successful, at times, for months; more often an unraveled failure within minutes—to blank the Six Million out of my mind.

When I first came to the United States in 1957, as an exchange
student and at the age of sixteen, I discovered that a four-year-old
might throw a plate of peas across a room and be no more than
mildly reprimanded, that milk did not need to be boiled on the day
it was purchased, that adults chewed gum. (I had received my first
stick of gum five years earlier, from an English soldier, on my way
home from school in a streetcar. He stood next to me in the aisle.
Just before getting off he turned toward me, looked past my left ear,
and thrust the gum at me. When I got home my mother slapped
me, had me throw out the wad, and—between sobs—made me

promise never to accept anything from a stranger again, particularly a foreigner, most particularly an occupation soldier.)

I discovered that pupils in high school did not sit in one room all day but surged through mammoth hallways past lockers with metal doors, which they slammed on their way to different rooms, once every hour. That boys and girls went to the same school and that girls wore ungainly socks in contrast to my Austrian peers and myself, who had worn stockings for years. At home I had come to feel comfortable with the foreign language in which I'd had six years of thrice-weekly lessons, working up from "the cat is on the mat" to Shakespeare. Now came the discovery that my English was not the anonymous raincoat I had fancied it to be: serviceable, a garment appropriate for a variety of alien climates, a measure of protective coloring allowing the foreigner beneath to pass among the natives without attracting undue attention. Instead I was obliged to flaunt the most restricted of wardrobes: language as outlandish apparel, gaudy, mismatched colors jarringly at odds with beige Shetland sweaters, an oddity impossible to overlook amid hundreds of identical jackets proclaiming my new school's name. Though I longed to disown my foreigner's garb I knew I needed it. I wrapped it tightly across my shoulders and clutched its fringed ends to my chest with both hands lest it slide off me during a moment of carelessness, leaving me mute, bereft even of this flimsy and garish shelter, my English, an improbably unfashion-able, loosely crocheted shawl, consisting of many more holes than thread. "Such big houses," I would say, but they were "tall buildings." One did not say "please" in response to "thank you," one said, "you are welcome," a phrase that, translated back into German, not only made no sense at all in a post–thank-you context but sounded comically, absurdly, like something Winnetou would say, my Sioux hero from the Karl May books that I had loved only a couple of years ago. Of course, my *Gymnasium* English lessons had been designed mainly to teach me to read. But even my confidence in the ability to decipher the written word was short-lived. "TaterTots" defied my dictionaries.

There were major discoveries, too. One occurred on a peaceful evening during one of the pleasant talks through which the American couple, who had offered to harbor a foreign student, now attempted to get to know this foreign student. They asked friendly questions that I answered happily, flattered by their attention and interest. I told them about my grandparents' mountain farm, about my scrappy twelve-year-old brother, and how important it was to my parents that I do well in school. And that my father had been building a house with his own hands, literally, year after year, every day after work and every weekend. It had taken him eight months to dig out the basement. Neighbors, marveling at the thickness of the homemade walls, had dubbed his project "Seiler's Bunker."

"Mom" and "Dad," as they had instructed me to call them, were delighted with this detail. "And he works at his job all day too, think of that," said Mom. And Dad asked, "Has he always worked as a clerk in a factory?"

"No," I said, "just for the last few years. Before that he worked as a laborer in that same factory and before that he was a locksmith, and before 1945 he was a policeman."

There was a silence, during which I smiled first at one, then at the other of the two adults facing me. "A policeman," repeated Dad. "You surely don't mean to say that your father was a *Nazi*."

"Yes," I said, "I think he was."

The questions that followed were put to me with a great deal more urgency: What rank had my father held, why had he never gone to prison, *had* he gone to prison? Where had he been during the war, how long had he been a policeman, how long had he been a Nazi, *what rank had he held*?

I was unable to answer any of these questions except one: No, he had never been to prison. Mom and Dad repeated the remaining questions and asked a number of others, but when my answers continued to be unsatisfactory the inquiries came to an end. "Nazis were evil," said Dad gravely.

"It's time to go to bed," said Mom.

"Right," said Dad. "Now we won't talk about any of this anymore, but National Socialism was evil and would have destroyed the world if we hadn't stopped it in time."

My second major discovery was television. Enjoyable as it was to watch the Mouseketeers with the four-year-old after school, dazzled as I was along with the family by Raymond Burr at night, nothing compared to what I came across three weeks into my stay. The set was kept upstairs, in a room next to the bedroom that I shared with the fifteen-year-old daughter of what was referred to as my "American family." Everyone was asleep. I quietly shut the door on the girl breathing deeply in the bed next to mine, moved a chair to within a foot of the set, and turned it on, very low, only to hear someone bark in German. An American actor, clearly, and mangling his lines so as to make me stifle a giggle and wonder whether my English appeared this comical to Americans. But linguistic concerns quickly became unimportant. When the make-believe German wearing a swastika armband had finished barking, he raised his rifle and struck a feeble old man on the head. The old man, whose hands were tied behind his back, collapsed at the attacker's feet, his face coming to rest, in close-up, partly on a cobblestone and partly on the kind of boots my father used to wear when I was a child.

So I had come upon my first war movie, to be followed by what seemed like hundreds. Throughout my stay I could count on seeing one nearly every night on one station or another, sometimes two in succession, sometimes—maddeningly—running concurrently. I would tiptoe downstairs and forage in the kitchen for oranges, a luxury I had not yet begun to take for granted. At home, in 1957, oranges were gifts for sick relatives confined to a hospital bed. The three daughters in this family drank juice and ate oranges under duress, their mother urging them: vitamin C. Along with oranges I brought up a package of Lorna Doone cookies. Then I sat, alternating a section of orange, a cookie, a section of orange, a cookie, twenty pounds gained in two months, my mouth moving, teeth chomping, brain absorbing, eyes riveted to a tiny screen on which images repeated themselves endlessly: monstrous Germans (or Austrians; the two were interchangeable), deviate, lurid, unspeakable. Rifle butts rammed into a prisoner's stomach, weeping civilians slaughtered, abominations overflowing three quarters of the movie's duration until good finally triumphed over evil. Sometimes the English or the French were there on the side of the good, or Oriental madmen joined the gang of evil. But most often it was Nazis against Americans and Americans won because they were noble and in the right.

Later a clergyman prayed, and while wolfing down the last piece of orange I watched flags, alive in the wind, and hummed the "Star-Spangled Banner" with my mouth full of crumbs scraped from this night's box of Lorna Doones. Then I crawled into bed, nauseous. The following night I would repeat the process, insatiable, and the night after that and the night after that. I did not understand half the English lines, but I understood the clatter of machine guns, and I concentrated on how ludicrously these supposed Germans mispronounced their mother tongue, in order to hold at bay a panic that cookies could not assuage.

Finally, there was an American History book belonging to Helen, who sat next to me in Algebra. She wore sweaters buttoned up the back and gloriously tight black skirts. Her name, in conjunction with a variety of boys' names, was embroidered in ball-point inside the front cover, underneath a stamp proclaiming the book to be the property of Eastwood High School. Having deciphered its title out of the corner of my eye, I wrote her a note asking if I might borrow the book for the duration of the period. Next day I sent her a similar note. From the third day on she handed me the book automatically until, three weeks later, she was transferred to a different class. At the end of the school year she handed me her history text, Helen & Bob/Jerry/Bill/Roy etc.

intact. "Keep it," she said. "I've never met anybody who was so crazy about a dumb schoolbook. But you're a sweet kid, don't forget me when you're back in Australia." I threw the book overboard the *Groote Beer*, an old Dutch battleship converted into a students' boat, between Montreal and Rotterdam, halfway home.

But for three weeks I studied the section on the Second World War. The first time around it took me four days to get all the way through, but soon I could read the chapter in a single period, undisturbed by the teacher writing numbers on a blackboard that in this country was green. I had neither oranges nor cookies at my disposal and held on to Helen's book instead, flexing my fingers once class was over and I was released to hurry on to Public Speaking.

Those were not "just" movies, then. The textbook dryly repeated, in essence if not in flamboyant detail, what I had already seen enacted: Nazi atrocities, Allied duty to end atrocities,

American victory. A bland textbook was in accord with my brutal midnight tutors. This war had not merely been one army's victory over another, it had been the victory of Good over Evil.

Every day after school I threw myself across the pink chenille spread on my bed and cried. The throwing-oneself-across-a-bed was a gesture I had read about in books, but the homesickness (for the way my father held a cigarette, how my mother pushed my hair off my forehead, for the ease with which my brother jumped off a moving streetcar, for myself as I had been only weeks ago) was real. It was also limited. I would sit up again and go to wash my face in the lush, pink bathroom that I shared with only one other person. And I would become engrossed in fussing with my hair, which had taken on a never-imagined importance in a country where girls washed theirs daily and spent many waking hours in curlers, a habit that astonished and delighted me. And I became engulfed in the myriad nuances—subtle enough to mystify and baffle a foreigner—of cotton socks and wool, and tennis shoes and saddle shoes and loafers, and where a pin was placed on a Peter Pan collar, and being one in a senior class of hundreds as opposed to the class I had left behind, and to which I would return, consisting of eighteen. And girls wearing boys' rings, and belonging to a sorority, sitting in a circle on the floor of someone's "family" room as opposed to a "living" room; trying to decode a process consisting of "reading the minutes" and "old business" and "new business" and potato chips and talk about girls who drink and girls who go all the way.

A new world indeed, increasingly attractive the better I found my way around in it. And throughout, the nightly forays on the refrigerator—not once did the woman I called Mom complain or ask; she merely replenished the stock of oranges and Lorna Doones and to this day I don't know what, if anything, she thought of their rapid disappearance—and the immersion into my reliably raging war. Two days before leaving I met a very recent Princeton graduate. Then the year was over.

I no longer have an accent. People I meet comment on that when they first hear that I grew up in Austria, and I am vain about it and love hearing the magic phrase, "But you don't have. . . ." Some consonants were tricky longer than others, the *v* in "elevator," for instance, and while I was teaching I had to be careful when I introduced "weak verbs." I was lucky with the initial letters *j* and *g*, pitfalls for many Austrians: Jell-O, German, jewelry, and ginger presented no obstacles. The one common English word that continues to be hazardous for me to pronounce—I have to concentrate a split second before saying it, each and every time—is Jew.

My mother cried and my father told me how proud he was of me and wanted, first off, to show me what progress he had made on the house during my absence. My brother had grown nearly two inches and had dismantled my bicycle, using its parts to fortify his own, which had blossomed into a much-endowed vehicle while mine was not to navigate again. And the first effort, three days into the homecoming, a question after dinner. "What was the war about?" And my father's calm reply, "I don't want to talk about it." And the same question and similar ones stretching over languid, end-of-summer evenings, when I would follow him to the *Grund*.

That's what we still called his nightly destination—"I'm going to the *Grund* now," "Is he back from the *Grund* yet?"—a holdover from the days when it was still a plot of land, before he had put up the provisional fence, and dug the provisional sewer, and connected the water, and put up the real fence, all along pacing out the floor plan again and again, until he was finally ready to ram a spade into the ground and begin the basement. *Grund* means "plot of land," also "earth," "soil," "reason," "motive," and "cause."

He was laying more bricks that summer, bent over his trowel in baggy old pants held up at the waist with a piece of string, sandals tied to his feet with more bits of string where leather straps had given way years ago, sweat running ribbons down the dusty skin under his arms.

I stood behind him, talking at his back. I had bathed in midafternoon in preparation for the nightly confrontation, and would wear a pair of white, patent-leather pumps and one of my pink Lady Bryant shirtwaist dresses, glamorous prizes from another continent, meant to lend to my interrogations the formality they deserved.

Not once did my father ask me to pass a trowel, or to hand him a brick, or to get him a tin cup of water. Nor did I offer to lift a finger. I stood up straight, tight-lipped and prim, the marrow of my bones turned to zeal.

As the sun went down my questions became louder. My father's answers stayed the same in tone and content, bland variations of his first reply. "You wouldn't understand," and "It's no use talking about it now." "Did you gas any Jews?" finally prompted a different answer, at dusk, on the last hot Sunday of the year. Carefully setting a brick into place on wet mortar, my father, enunciating as one does one month into a beginners' foreign language course, said, "If you care to leave my house, forever, right now, you need only repeat what you just said." I did not care to leave his house. But the following evening I asked in a raised voice, "Do you have any idea what the Americans say—do you?" and my father said, without looking up, "If you want to believe the pap the Americans feed you, go ahead." "I don't *want* to believe them," I cried, "tell me your side, tell me *our* side," and he said, "It's too late."

My mother kept repeating, "How I wish you had never gone over there, we thought it would be a wonderful opportunity for you, we should never have let you go. Don't upset your father, he knows what he's doing, be grateful, why do you upset him so, think about his ulcers." "His ulcers, my God," I would yell; yelling at her was permissible. "Do you know what the Nazis *did*? There were concentration camps right here in Austria, how come there aren't any Jews around, none in my school, none in this neighborhood, did every last one get knocked off? I want to know what he had to do with that, it's my right!"

And my gentle, always sickly, overweight, and overworked mother, who cried often and easily—at newspaper headlines: Lost Toddler Found Safe in Neighbor's Yard—would say, dry-eyed, fierce, "No. If your father chooses not to talk about something, *that* is a right. You have no right whatsoever. *He is your father.*"

A true Austrian—"facts are facts," "that's how it is," "what you can't change you live with"—I kept at it for no longer than two weeks. After that I concentrated on how satisfyingly Graz rye bread stills the vaguest appetite, the fiercest hunger; how the fog, that autumn, would drift through my hometown's streets, while the tops of surrounding hills glowed bright by midmorning; how my brother, day by day, became less the stranger he had been at the airport, if not yet a friend an ally, handsome, too—I had never thought of him in terms of looks—with his easy, brash toughness among peers, his brittle, guarded lack of either amiability or its opposite around my father; and how my mother would look at me, sideways, and how those glances soon were no longer expressions of fear alone (fear for me? for herself? for him? for us?) but mixed with a sort of pride, a hint of "my daughter, who has been to America." And I concentrated on schoolwork, of which there was a large amount to make up, back again in a quiet room with eighteen desks, students and teachers familiar to me since the age of ten. I told a few stories about America when other girls reported on their summer vacations, and tried to pretend to myself it had all been no more than the type of holiday my classmates were accustomed to every year: the south of France, or St. Moritz, or, at the very least, northern Italy.

My mother looks up from the magazine she is reading. "Will you look at the picture of this pretty Swedish girl, she is marrying an African. He's black as coal, how can she do this to her poor family?"

My parents spoke openly about their distrust of blacks and abhorred the idea of "mingling" with them, though there was no chance of that in Graz. For whatever reason, their example did not affect me the way my parents intended. Blacks don't haunt me. Like men, they are "other" and there. I love this one, don't like that one, give little thought to most. Jews are a different story. Yet as often and as diligently as I have sifted through my brain, I cannot remember my parents, my teachers, my friends—anyone while I was growing up—saying a word about Jews. Not pro, not con, not ever.

In order to graduate with my class, a goal inordinately important to me, I had to make up my lost academic year by Christmas. Public Speaking was of no help, nor was American History. My English had improved, of course, but English was only one subject among thirteen. They had done Central and South America in Geography, had read vast material in German class, I could no longer keep up with what they were doing in Latin, French, Chemistry, and Physics. Math seemed hopeless. "Well, Seiler," our math teacher said on the first day of school before a hushed class, "I hope you had a pleasant time. Better hang on to those memories—skyscrapers and whatnot—because you'll flunk my course, you've always been stupid in math."

They had conquered calculus while I had learned about the importance of being asked to football games and the victory of Good over Evil, and my prospects were poor. But a math student at the University of Graz bicycled to our apartment at the outskirts of town every evening to coach me. It was a major effort for which my parents paid him a very small sum, while I accompanied him to several Sunday morning symphony concerts.

Throughout the year, the now-not-so-recent Princeton graduate back in the United States wrote romantic letters to me. I was happy to receive them and answered each one. A month after I had graduated from the *Erstes Bundesrealgymnasium für Mädchen* (being nearly physically aware of how the principles of calculus melted from my brain) he came to Austria. We sat on a park bench surrounded by roses when he told me he intended to marry me. That evening he formally asked my father for my hand.

My father said no, she has to go to college first, and the young American said, I give you my word I'll put her through school myself. My mother cried and repeated at length that America did not have socialized medicine and what if she gets sick, and the young American promised to take out more than an adequate amount of health insurance.

I said little and my brother said nothing. He sat behind the kitchen table eating peanuts from a large china bowl, looking at whoever was speaking, winking at me whenever the others were talking at once. Each time the negotiations reached an impasse he halted the cracking of shells, as if he saw his contribution to the proceedings to consist of keeping humdrum noises under control. And the idea of getting married seemed lovely to me, and my suitor struck me as romantic and valiant, argue as he did with my father. Besides, how contrary to all the books I had read on the subject, that this man had not asked me to marry him, but had merely stated his intention; here was a man who knew what he wanted. What I wanted was to get out.

Austria, my family, had transmuted from home-taken-for-granted into a vicious undertow. Nothing, so I was convinced at the time, will ever be explained to me *here*. Whatever sucks at me with such force will continue to be unnamed, unspeakable. It will suck at me and suck and suck some more and will not stop until I am back where I belong, where I was less than two years ago, when Syracuse was a Greek city, not automatically followed by an appendage, an amalgam said in one breath: Syracuse New York. The exchange student had returned a changeling, its crib someone else's, the comfort it found in this foreign crib meant for the child "snatched," as Austrian folklore had it, "by the Gypsies." Out then, to find and rejoin whatever unknown tribe had put me into a foreigner's, an Austrian child's crib, warm and close though it was and smelling of chamomile, its sides at times indistinguishable from my skin, my mother's skin, my father's. What I wanted and needed was to get out.

So we were married and spent close to a decade in small Midwestern towns. My husband, who loved me and who was a man of his word, did indeed put me through school, driving me to class every morning and picking me up again in the late afternoon, uncomplainingly, for the years it took until I graduated once more, having fulfilled my history requirement by taking a course called "Intellectual Survey of Western Civilization," which stayed away from the Second World War entirely. And we had two children. A girl first, it gave me deep pleasure to choose her name, Ursula, a traditional Austrian name backed up by a saint for good measure. And I was busy, content, and most often happy, although the second child, the boy, had been ill at birth and stayed ill.

I taught German in high school, where I borrowed another American History book, this one from one of my juniors. It was marked, discreetly and only on the first page, Amy & Walt. The book's perusal more than sufficed for my citizenship examination, which consisted of two questions: Who is the governor of Wisconsin? And: Who freed the slaves? A month later I swore that I had never been nor was then a Communist, and that I had never supported myself either through illegal gambling or prostitution. Another month after that I swore that during the four weeks since my last oath I again had been neither Communist, prostitute, nor gambler, and became an American citizen.

A few years later I fell deeply in love with a man very different from the one I had married, and left my husband. My father wrote me an anguished letter, telling me about his sorrow, reminding me that his grandchildren would now grow up without a proper set of parents, that marriage was a commitment no one in our family had ever reneged on, and that he felt personally implicated: I was rejecting not only my own choice, but one of which he had approved. The letter ended with the sentence, "If you do not return to your husband immediately, I shall never speak to you again."

My mother, though deeply upset, did continue to write to me after the divorce. More than anything she wanted me to come home, so that her grandson could be treated by Austrian doctors. The dilemma was that while he could have been taken care of for free by Austria's exemplary socialized-medicine machine, there was also the fact that this apparatus did not, at the time, perform kidney transplants, while America's nonsocialized medical machinery did them as a matter of course. What's more, when my son's money-conscious doctor first told me that a transplant would be necessary within a year, he added this suggestion: "Your insurance probably won't cover that—dependents' transplants are a little esoteric. Even if you could get the money together, through loans or whatever, you'd be in debt for decades. So why don't you go on welfare? You're divorced, two kids, one's always sick, you won't have any trouble at all."

I quit my job and did as advised, and within a year—Mark was seven—one of my kidneys had been slipped into place in my son's small abdomen. The transplant was faultless, a success. However, Mark's heart gave up three weeks later.

My father, who had made good on his word not to speak to me, held firm. There was no response from him to my telegram telling him about the death of his grandson. Seven months later my mother died of cancer; my father, four months after that, of a heart attack.

I am reading *Adolf Hitler* by John Toland. It's my very first effort at tackling this massive subgenre of literature, this Hitler-market fodder, and the going is tedious. Every step, every half step, every two-inch shuffle of history is set forth with equally loving patience. I am on page 307, alternately squeezing my eyes shut and opening them wide, in an effort to stay awake: ". . . far beyond the required two-thirds majority with 441 for the bill, 94 against—the National Socialists leaped to their feet cheering . . . then with hands outstretched they sang the 'Horst Wessel Song':

"Raise high the flags! Stand rank and rank together,
Storm troopers march with steady, quiet tread. . . ."

Jesus, I think, bored and irritated, what a harebrained song—
that must have been quite a melody to go with "rank and rank"
and "steady tread"—but in mid-thought my forehead breaks out
in sweat. *"Die Fahnen hoch,"* someone croons, *"die Reihen fest
geschlossen . . ."* words devoid of meaning, a familiar succession
of vowels and softly smudged Austrian consonants, "SA
marschiert . . ." intensely, powerfully moving. There's no need
for me to wonder about the melody. I know the melody, *". . . mit
ruhigem, festen Schritt,"* a lovely melody, simple as the folk songs
my mother used to hum while peeling potatoes.

So did she hum this one, too? I sit up straight and try to read
some more and can't. I dial the first two digits of a friend's number,
then remember it's three in the morning and spitefully drop the
receiver into its cradle from a height of two feet, watch it jump,
listen to it clatter. I rotate my head, brushing each shoulder with
my chin and cheeks in turn. The maneuvers don't work. I am
shaken as one is shaken when a brick lands on a sidewalk, missing
one's head by a hundredth of a second, by a tenth of an inch. I am
helplessly beside myself, enraged: What the *hell* is going on, where
the *hell* did this come from, who the *hell* sang this song to me and
when, when, when?

Nobody in Austria sang the "Horst Wessel Lied" after 1945. So
it must have been before then. Was I one and a half? Two? Three?
How can a song pop up like that, words and melody complete, and
not just any song, either! What *is* all this junk mired in my brain,
hovering, and why can't it come out, finally, all in one lump,
or stay away from me, leave me alone, leave me? "SA
marschiert. . . ." Who lulled me to sleep with songs about
marching storm troopers, before the age of four?

I don't remember how old I was when I first became aware of having an Uncle Eduard. Trying to recall what words were used to describe him ("he is out of our lives," "we don't mention his name," "that unspeakable, that no-good bum") I realize I am merely fabricating phrases.

There was, at any rate, an uncle who owned a bakery in a village near the one in which he had been born. He had gone to America as a young man and had promised his favorite younger brother that he would send for him. Eduard had not "kept his word." My betrayed father died true to *his* word, not to speak to his older brother again.

In August 1977, during one of my visits to Austria, my brother and I sent him a card: We are your niece and nephew and would like to visit you next Sunday.

We had no idea whether Uncle Eduard would even let us into his house. There had been no answer to the card. Our visit was a lark to us, a minor adventure. My brother driving too fast, telling jokes during the ride through the countryside: vineyards, tobacco fields, potato patches, the farmhouses closing in upon themselves, built around a central courtyard, scrabbling chickens and women hanging up laundry hidden from outsiders.

He must have done all right. In the tradition of his village those who did all right in America returned to Austria. Those who did not stayed away, abandoned their families, vanished. Without admitting it to myself I expected an aged pirate, a grizzly renegade, the only family member besides myself to brave the New World. Had he traveled widely? Had he had a high time? Had he been to California, Alaska, New York? Conceivably he had fathered cousins of mine (a woman with my nose and chin, a man with my brother's eyebrows) who now lived unbeknown to me in Manhattan, around the corner, up the street.

It was a sweltering afternoon, the village lay deserted, the shutters were closed on the bakery with his last name on a large sign. It thrilled me—extraordinarily, excessively—to see it spelled out like this, in public, my name too for half my life. And there he was, a fragile old man who cried throughout nearly our entire visit in his narrow, low-ceilinged kitchen.

A distant relative, settling an old debt, had paid his passage. "What a stroke of luck, a great stroke of luck, America!" He had been homesick on his first day and during the ensuing weeks and months, but had assumed that the gnawing pain would disappear or at least lessen with time. It did not. After two years as a baker's assistant in a town in New York State he gave up and went home.

"I couldn't eat. The homesickness made my body ache during the day and at night I couldn't sleep." After a few months at home he recovered his health, spent his American savings on yet another crossing, and worked in the same bakery for three more years until, again, he was too ill to continue. He went home, recovered, and returned to Binghamton, New York, to bake more bread, rolls, cakes, and doughnuts. After eight years and three starts he had saved enough money to buy into a small bakery at home. He had understood no English when he arrived in America and spoke very little when he left for good. He had scrimped miserably for eight years, he had made no friends. "It was the worst time of my life." During the first few years he had been unable to scrape together the money for my father's fare; later he had become determined that no one in his family should know how poorly he lived.

Either/or, yes/no, black/white. Though I know such reactions well, finally, at the age of thirty-eight, all too often I cannot react differently.

This slavery held my father captive all his life. No adjusting, no reconsidering, no slow disillusioning, no flexibility possible. A brother makes a promise and does not keep it—the reason is beside the point—is never to be spoken to again. A daughter who does not respond to her father's demand to continue her marriage is no longer a daughter, and no matter what happens in her life, an undaughter stays dead. Former Nazi cops, dismissed along with my father in 1945, who are financially wise and politically astute and who possibly regret having been National Socialists, return a decade later to a police force that is ready to pardon and reinstate them. They are no longer among my father's acquaintances, he himself declines the invitation to return to the force. Not because he still sees himself as a Nazi, not out of disregard for the police of Austria's Second Republic, or for financial gain—he would have been far better paid as a cop—but from the conviction that a man of worth upholds only one *Weltanschauung* per life. Should this one creed go, as his did, a search for a new one was out of the question; all that remained was making do without a creed.

For a lifetime my father lived as if driven by a machine with only an on/off switch governing emotion and brain, a switch, moreover, that worked only once for any human being or idea. There is a beloved brother, and then he is not. And he is not from then on—for one decade, for five, still not spoken to by a man of sixty-six because of a disappointment suffered half a century before. An inability to see any matter from another person's point of view, not a refusal, an inability. An extreme world, none of the nuances of a more evolved manner of dealing with one's life's events, no shades of gray or mauve. Clear-cut, and the crippling cost in pain accepted as inevitable. All depths of disappointment can be suffered, all measures of loneliness endured, a man keeps his word. That's what he died with, all those kept words.

My son's death could not break my father's silence and I watched my uncle cry, an old man recounting how a lifelong separation had come about. Both times, so it seems to me, my father was clearly and hurtfully "in the wrong." Yet the clarity of my response becomes muddled when I look at the social equivalents to his private rigidities. His refusal, for instance, to reenter the police force after the prescribed decade of repentance, a police force that had, of course, proclaimed the absolute evil of the police force it replaced. His refusal to announce, if only by implication, "What I stood for was all wrong." Something in me cannot but say, good for him. No matter what else he was, that man never lied, he stuck to his guns.

"Sticking to one's guns"—no wonder a military expression is apt. How asinine, asinine! But there is this thrill in me, nonetheless, this satisfaction: He never lied. Would it not have been the greater courage by far to repent, to renounce having been a Nazi? Yes, says my brain, of course. They all should have deeply repented, including my father. (And a snide little side-thought sidles up to my moral conviction: It was certainly wiser to repent, publicly of course, or at any rate to lie, if one intended to continue to live and work in Austria.)

But what if you were heartsick with all that had eventually turned up, repelled and heartsick to the core with what it had all turned into, but convinced that how you had originally seen it *yourself*, that what you had believed in *yourself*, had been fine and honorable? Are you heartsick but proclaim, at the same time, that you have never been a part of it? What do you do, in such a case?

What most of them did was to crawl on their bellies and lie. Most of those millions of Nazis crossed their hearts six times a day and bleated, "I was never one of them," "I saw through it from the start," "I was against it all along," "They made me join." Like the man in our neighborhood, formerly an important Nazi, who made a smooth transition in 1945, enabling him to advance in rank and be a policeman again, immediately, under the new regime. "The *Herr Major*," Mrs. Lehmann says to my mother under her breath, turning down one corner of her mouth. "Watch my words, when the Chinese and the Swedes get together and occupy Austria he'll prove to us all how he fought in the Swedish-Chinese underground as a tot, and he'll be *Herr General* for them." My mother glances at me and says nothing.

The *Polizeisiedlung*—police settlement—was one of the building projects with which Hitler intended to revive Austria's economy. When the war was over, half of the cops, who had been given apartments in those brand-new buildings, were ordered to vacate half the rooms in their apartments so that the remaining half of former cops' families could be moved in with them. The buildings freed in this manner were taken over by occupation forces.

By 1955, when those occupation forces left, English families had lived a couple of apartment buildings away from mine for two thirds of my life, and my classmates and I had studied English three times a week for four years. Not once did it occur to us to connect these studies with the fact that native speakers of the language abounded in town.

Except for taunts, shouted from behind laundry posts, there was no connection possible. Austrian children did not play with English children, Austrian mothers did not speak to English mothers, Austrian fathers ignored English fathers. There was nothing directly reminiscent of the war in the occupation of our neighborhood except, of course, for the foreign uniforms. The troops were stationed in barracks clear across town, there were no tanks lumbering down the streets of our project. English officers and their families lived in apartment buildings in which Austrians had lived before them and with which all of us were familiar. All buildings in the project were constructed alike, identical rooms laid out identically, the same narrow wooden balconies, the same staircases. When the English tenants moved in they must have seen the basements still outfitted as they commonly were before they made the sudden transition from being the most essential part of any building back again to being merely useful: crude wooden bunk beds, assorted gas masks, water buckets, the furnishings of emergency air-raid shelters for families unable to reach the fortified public bunkers in time. When the English dismantled these basements to make room for prams and folded lawn chairs and tool kits and spare bicycle tires, did they relish an image of cowering Austrians awaiting English bombers? Or did they recall huddling in similarly equipped shelters awaiting German *Stukas?* Did they compare blackout measures, emergency exits? Did they keep a *Wehrmacht* gas mask as a souvenir?

For ten years they lived next door, yet they did not exist. My chewing-gum episode was my one contact with the occupation forces. The English children weren't children, less popular or more so, kids to be wooed or liked or tolerated or communally castigated. They were our height and size and width but they were not there, one averted one's eyes. No, one looked straight ahead.

"I don't believe it," says Mrs. Lehmann. She is at our kitchen window, her elbows on the solid, sausage-shaped pillow covered in gray-and-white-striped mattress ticking that slumps along the length of our windowsill to keep out drafts. She beckons to my mother with a yellow forefinger. My mother completes the row on her knitting machine, carefully lays the ball of yarn that has been on her lap onto the kitchen table, and joins Mrs. Lehmann. I sidle up behind them.

It is an icy January afternoon. Below, two boys (one behind the other, their heads bent) walk past our building through fine snow that is being slashed into giants' sheets by a fierce wind. "Look at their knees," says Mrs. Lehmann and lets out a clucking sound and a slow whistle accompanied by a shake of the head.

The boys hurry down my street wearing gray caps, not knitted but made of fabric and leaving their ears exposed, foreign caps. And jackets and long socks. Their gray trousers stop directly above the knees.

"Blue!" says Mrs. Lehmann. "Their scrawny little knees are blue! They can't even dress their kids. How can a mother, even if she's English, let a ten-year-old out of the house like that in this cold, how stupid can you be."

"They won the war," says my mother, turning back to her knitting. "They can't all be stupid."

A small group has gathered around one editor's desk. We are drinking white wine out of Styrofoam cups, engaged in our favorite topic—how swamped we are with work. The "host" editor, half-buried behind wire baskets piled to the toppling point, declares that she will not, will *not*, come into the office again this weekend. "And another thing," she says. "I just read three manuscripts in a row about growing up Jewish in Brooklyn. We've been buying too much Jewish stuff lately. I bet it doesn't even reflect our readership. Besides, it's getting to be a drag."

The speaker is highly accomplished at her craft, sharply

intelligent, efficient, classically WASP attractive, one of the two or three most respected editors at the magazine. Her tone and demeanor have been as unselfconscious as if she had just announced that the front of the book needs to be cut by three and a half pages.

"So-and-so's piece wasn't that hot anyway, let's kill it. Is there any more wine?" says the woman to my right and drains her cup.

"No, that was it," says another, winding her watch. "Let's not order from that place again, it took them an hour to get one bottle up here. And who wants to reflect a readership, anyway? Does anybody want to share a cab?"

"Aw, you're all full of shit," yawns a third. "When was the last Jewish anything we ran? I bet you can't even remember. I'm ordering some more, I've got to stay and do boards, and it's Friday night."

I, too, have read those three manuscripts. The articles happen to overlap in content, message, tone, and style. When manuscripts nearly duplicate one another, it is an editor's sometimes difficult job to choose the best of the lot, and her always unpleasant responsibility to reject the rest. Yet I could no more make such a selection in this case, or even voice an opinion on this matter—an *editorial* matter—than I could will myself to become left-handed overnight. Nor would this Austrian Nazi's daughter comment on an alleged disproportionate number of manuscripts addressed to, or written by, Jews. "Disproportionate" as compared to what, compared to whom? How does a Nazi's daughter address a matter of "proportions" when Jews are involved, whatever the case, instance, specific topic? This particular Austrian Nazi's daughter loses any editorial judgment she may generally have at her command when faced with a matter involving "proportions" and "Jews." She feels she has forfeited the right to objectivity in such a matter, forfeited the right to any opinion whatever on such a matter, forfeited by virtue of parentage.

All of this, of course, was my perspective, mine alone. Not once during my four years at that magazine did I broach such topics with any of my colleagues. For all I know, some of them might have happily disabused me of the notion that they considered me, foremost, a Nazi's daughter. For all I know, some, or many, or most of my Jewish colleagues were far too busy, or just as self-absorbed as I was, to take the time to give any thought to what they knew of my background. I have no idea. No one at the magazine mentioned my country to me, except possibly in terms of the Salzburg *Festspiele*, skiing conditions, having once, as a college sophomore, camped near Innsbruck. I have no idea if, and if so to what degree, my colleagues thought of me as the offspring of a Nazi—a term commonly used in our office as a synonym for "murderer," "killer," "slaughterer of children," "evil incarnate." I do not know what either my Jewish or my Christian colleagues thought of my heritage, because they did not venture, and I refrained from soliciting, an opinion.

On that particular Friday night I crimped a fluted design into the rim of my cup, waiting for my face to cool, hoping to remain unnoticed until I could regain my composure. I was deeply envious. Just like that, I thought; she can come out with such a comment just like that.

So there was Austria's Second Republic, the government put together after the war, awash with citizens who had never had anything to do with the Nazis. Where had they all disappeared to, those 99.75 percent of Austrians who had voted for the *Anschluss*, for Hitler? Granted all the reasons advanced for voting "yes" while hating Nazis—envelopes containing the votes were stacked neatly on the desks of election officials and it might have been possible to trace names to specific votes—one did not vote "no" because one feared retaliation; or one voted "yes," hoping to appease the Germans in order to prevent the worst; or the *Anschluss* was already a fact, one's single vote would not have changed reality. . . . *But 99.75 percent?*

And after the war there were enough people to set up shop again, to take over not just cabinet posts but a full-scale network of government jobs, held not merely by repentant Nazis or not-any-more Nazis but, most of them, by a brand-new stereotype: the never-having-been-a-Nazi politician, judge, policeman, teacher, clerk, streetcar conductor.

There is a difference between saying, It turned into a monstrous crime, I have changed my heart and mind and want to pick up the pieces and start a new and different life, and saying, It was dreadful, wasn't it? Criminal! Luckily, I was never part of it, look here, I couldn't stand him all along, I was one of those 0.25 percent who voted "no" way back then, neatly stacked envelopes never bothered *me.*

Not once did my father say, "I had nothing to do with it." How things had come about was beyond his grasp, but it was clear that what he had believed in had turned vile, vile to him as well as to the world. That he was unable, even in retrospect, to explain to himself exactly *what* had happened, rendered him politically speechless. From 1945 on, any comment about parties, movements, or politicians was cut short by my father with the sentence, "They are all alike." (There was one exception. In 1956 or 1957, one evening after dinner, my mother announced to the table at large that she had voted for the Socialists that day. "I've thought a lot about it," she said, "and the Reds do more . . ." here she lifted her chin in her husband's direction, ". . . for him than the others do," and then she blushed. It may have touched him that she so clearly felt she had behaved adventurously. He greeted her announcement with a mock widening of the eyes and a smile, swallowed his last sip of coffee, patted her arm, and said, "I'm going to the *Grund* now, I'll be home by ten.")

But in the summer of 1945 he hid in the countryside and then took up, at the age of thirty-nine, where he had left off as an adolescent, working for a locksmith. And abruptly—desperately, indiscriminately—began to sleep with as many women as would have him, causing his ill wife deep grief. And bathed his ill wife daily, tending her with rare devotion. And scrubbed the public staircase in our apartment building when it was our family's turn, because it was of great importance to his bedridden wife not to have "any talk" about how the Seilers did not pull their weight in this communal mania for immaculate stairs, though he knew that this amounted, among the men in the building, to his irreparable loss of face. And went on to organize and conduct a factory band and a factory orchestra at night, alternately rehearsing the two groups for concerts held before family members of the factory musicians, after working as a laborer during the day. And worked to numbing exhaustion daily, skimping, skimping, no more than one beer a month allowed, until he was able to buy, by dint of extreme self-denial, the cheapest and weediest lot on the outskirts of Graz.

And worked every night from then on, on that lot, abandoning affairs and factory orchestras, having settled on a house for his children as the core of his remaining life. And did not once mention to his children, as other fathers did, casually, that National Socialism had, after all, one mustn't forget, in those early years, of course, had its good points. He renounced his obsession in his heart. But he was neither mercurial enough to renounce it publicly nor flexible or wise enough to renounce it to his children. And he was too proud to claim those mitigating circumstances of time, economy, and place, which he might have cited as well as the millions who made such a point of citing them. He made no excuses, he never lied, and his arrogance cows and thrills me.

I lie often and easily. Faced with a friend's work that I find mediocre I murmur, "This is really *something*," and whenever I don't want to see someone I say, "I would love to, but unfortunately I've already . . ." I lie to myself about why I lie to others, refusing the clarity of cowardice as motive, calling lies a form of tact instead. I have to start over on nearly every page I write because the urge to improve on facts is strong and ever-present. And I lie to myself when I am afraid to live with a truth. Wearing a new dress and high heels in a taxi on my way to a restaurant and in a good mood, I tell myself, You are finally over Mark's death. My brain is a pushover for lies; only my body insists on the truth. Out of the corner of my eyes I see a small boy running down the sidewalk, one sneaker has come untied and he has light hair; a fist plunges into my stomach, I lay my forehead on my knees and crouch on the plastic seat, and for the next few days I dare not deceive myself. But a week later there is that thought again, it flits from brain cell to brain cell . . . behind you . . . over.

But what was there to be done? Once the war was over, Austrians and occupiers alike knew that few of those strident claims of noninvolvement could be anywhere near the truth. Yet what was there to be done about it? Some Nazis were shot. Others were first tried and then shot, or tried and hanged. Others were imprisoned, fined, barred from holding jobs. That left—how many? And if they'd *all* been shot or imprisoned, who was going to run either the country or the streetcars? There was chaos. Graz, as a typical Austrian city, had had 42 percent of its housing destroyed by bombs; cadavers, human and animal, lay rotting in the streets.

Only the fortunate were living on seven hundred calories a day; in cities rations had sunk to eighty calories. Thousands starved. Somebody would have to work, a lot of somebodies would have to work, and others would have to tell them where to start and what to do.

The Communists were ready to rule. They had earned their laurels as foes of Fascism and did indeed get a third of the posts doled out to them in the provisional postwar government. They lost them again, miserably, six months later, as a result of the first elections. Women voted heavily in those elections, and the particular brutality with which the Russian army had occupied its sector of Austria was remembered at the polls: row upon row of women in front of every Vienna clinic, awaiting first aid after having been raped, others lying motionless on hallway cots in wretchedly crowded hospitals; a couple of months later, ecclesiastical dispensations granted, women waiting once more in dreary lines, this time for abortions. Missing in those lines were raped nuns, required by the Church to bear their children.

After those elections, the Russians, who had eagerly helped establish the provisional government, fought this very government point for point, step by step. Originally it had been the Americans' turn to be chagrined. Their idea of a new Austrian government was not one established in Vienna during the weeks when the Russians were sole occupiers of that city; the West was becoming familiar with the political makeup of governments set up under the supervision of Russian tanks.

It was the beginning of a fierce and extraordinarily tedious struggle between the superpowers, occasioned by Austria's misfortune of position, lying on the middle of a line that divides Europe's East from Europe's West, from the Baltic to the Adriatic; which is why I lived from the age of five to the age of fifteen in a tiny country occupied by its former enemies, who claimed to be friends, but who needed to stick around, in uniform, over and over again discussing Austria's fate around Austrian dining-room tables, unable to rouse themselves and go home. It took ten years to settle the score, with Austria the pawn. The Russians fought with trucks of grain, ideology, and the promise of terror. The Americans fought with money and won.

But that was later. In December 1945 there were, aside from the Communists, quickly reduced again to an insignificant fraction, some leftover Conservatives—who, for a start, changed their organization's name from the Christian Social Party to the Austrian People's Party—and there were some Socialists, too. Dr. Karl Renner, for instance, who had been the first chancellor of the First Austrian Republic after the First World War, a man in his seventies who had been living peacefully and comfortably by virtue of the fact that his own brand of Socialism was so right wing that the Nazis had had no qualms about him. "Is that old traitor still alive? He's just the man we need," Stalin is supposed to have said. Counting on this white-haired patriarch as a symbol of reassurance to a people who had just been through the collapse of its Fascist regime and was about to be governed by a regime as Communist as the presence of the Soviet army could guarantee, the Russians had plucked Dr. Renner from retirement and had made him chancellor of the new, Second, Republic. What the Russians wanted from this chancellor was what they wanted from figureheads they had installed in provisional governments all over Eastern Europe: that he should tire easily, look dignified, and keep his mouth shut.

Dr. Renner did look dignified. I remember him, if vaguely, because he presided over my elementary school rooms. A dusty black-and-white photograph, hung very high, too high for a seated child to distinguish features clearly, hung too high and next to the obligatory cross, equally dusty, equally remote. "We lost the war," says a teacher, "and now the enemy occupies our defeated country." "Occupy?" "To use." "Who is the country?" "All of us." "*I* am not a defeated country," says one girl. "My name is Liselotte Gerber, and I live on Bayernstrasse." "Bayernstrasse is in Graz and Graz is in Austria." "But, but . . ." says the girl, "I'll fight." "The war is over. Those soldiers carrying guns? They are the victors." "I wasn't in the war," says the girl, and another one blurts out, "My father was a brave soldier and he used to have a gun." "Mine, too," says a third. "Mine too, mine too," say a fourth and a fifth. "Yes, well," says the teacher, "not anymore."

Dr. Renner wore a neat white beard and his dusty face under glass was framed in black, like the photographs next to obituary notices in Austrian newspapers. When the sun shone into the room at a particular angle, the reflection obliterated him and only the shapes were left, a black cross and a rectangle framing nothing.

Under Dr. Renner's beard we studied from books that had blank labels glued across the lower part of the front page. Forbidden to touch those labels, we picked and picked at them nonetheless. Long before the end of the first month of school, many of our labels were no longer securely affixed. Between the end of one school year and the beginning of the next, someone pasted fresh blanks into all the books.

I wonder who actually did the work—our hapless teachers? Sitting in an empty classroom, flies buzzing in the summer heat, a pot of glue before you and around you piles of books; replacing frazzled labels with crisp, white ones, hoping to hide the swastika imprints from yet another batch of six-year-olds.

Our adults, those creatures unlike us, those creatures who knew what to do, who had led us safely into bomb shelters, and who were now teaching us to read, those adults had made a mistake. What's more, it was a mistake they did not want us to know about. So they blanked it out, year after year after year, until a book was tattered and gray except for its bright-white sticker up front, a drop of glue congealed in one corner, ooze arrested in mid-escape. Our adults were adamant about their stickers. Yet the rule against picking was enforced by a flat scolding—an apathetic scolding compared, for example, to the kind of scolding expected by a pupil who talked while the teacher talked, or stood up too slowly when the principal entered the room. It was a rule, no whimsy, but there was something halfhearted about it just the same, and something muggy. The sight of a small, purple-ink cross, four little legs bent at right angles, chased our adults into speaking rapidly and in a tight voice: "They were stamps of another government, we now have a new government, we will now learn the names of the rivers and streams of East Styria."

"Das schwartze Mädchen" occurs in a manuscript. To verify the spelling a researcher comes to me, the magazine's authority on German. " 'Schwartze' is wrong," I say. "There's no *t.*" "Oh, really?" is the reply. "Actually, I just wanted to check the dots on 'Mädchen.' So-and-so knows Yiddish, and she already said 'schwartze' is okay." "Maybe in Yiddish it is," I say, slowly and pedantically. "But in German it's 'schwarze,' and since the scene takes place in Stuttgart and the remark is made by a Stuttgarter pointing out a black girl, I assume we are dealing with German." "Okay, then," says the woman from research cheerfully. "As long as you're sure, that's good enough for me," and leaves. *Yiddish,* something hisses inside me, seething, ferocious. *How I detest it, pidgin German, a sickening bastardization of my beautiful-beautiful-language-my-home-my-language-my-beautiful-beautiful* —and catch myself, terrified. I have, once again, been sitting at my desk, over an unseen manuscript, on the eleventh floor above Lexington and Forty-first, spinning off.

When I first moved into my current one-room apartment I pretended that this was my living room, and that my closet door opened onto a hallway, at the end of which any number of spacious rooms might await my perusal. This conceit demands the camouflage of one's bed so as to make it appear, if not an essential part of a living room, at least not too obvious a piece of bedroom furniture. A fold-out sofa, of course, is ideal. But even without such a sofa, various friends of mine in their equally small apartments manage to conceal what they sleep on. I never could. No matter how I placed my twin-size cot, coffee table and arm chairs obstinately grouped themselves around this obvious . . . bed.

Then a friend offered me a king-size, four-poster extravaganza. I got rid of what furniture there was except for a desk and a chair and accepted her offer.

Since a king-size bed is impossible to conceal in a twelve-by-seventeen-foot room, it made sense to acknowledge that my apartment was now a bedroom. Over the ensuing months and years I added wallpaper and curtains and dark blue carpeting, a dark blue blanket, ruffled pillow shams, and gilt frames around photographs of my family and friends.

Now I wake up each day with a start: What does any of this have to do with me?

A bulletin board covers one wall, stretching in sections across the closet door to the cubicle that is the kitchen. I have tacked up labeled cards, beginning with 1906, my father's birth, continuing, one label per year, until 1955, where I ran out of space. This rhinoceros of a board needs to be on my wall so that I may get even a minimal grasp on my parents' lives. I can't, simply cannot, make myself remember how old my parents were in any given year, or where they were, or what they were doing, always in relation to what was happening at large in a country that was a caldron: swirling its people up or under, drowning them or having them ride a red-hot crest, leaving no one undisturbed.

The great gift that the country I now live in dispenses as a matter of course—the luxury of being allowed to choose a private life—was not available to my parents' generation. Ah, spare me their fate. Let me just do my work and love my daughter and a few friends, let me live out my life in this lush state of grace, not to be involved. Let the topic of morning conversations be the weather or the Yankees, not where the city was hit during the night, my mother dragging me past rubble, air thick with smoke and the odor of charred flesh; let not one of the foreign voices I hear for the rest of my life be that of a soldier of an enemy army; let the idea of victors and vanquished apply to Democrats and Republicans or vice versa, let politics be pedestrian and useful, let those with aspirations to greatness rub themselves raw in New York's art world and be barred from all politics; if they had admitted ambitious Adolf into their precious Academy of Arts he might have been just another architect, Vienna could have put up with any number of pompous-ass buildings. . . .

My blue-and-white bedroom is unrecognizable. The dark blue blanket, the dark blue rug, all my surfaces are covered with red, red-on-black, black-on-red, art directors who design the covers of Hitler books like red and black. My sanctuary invaded, swastikas everywhere. On book jackets, on forty-year-old newspapers, on record covers and official documents, precise lightning gashes zigzag around me.

I'll make covers for all the books, I think, one morning at four, brown-shopping-bag covers like those I loved making in grade school. But I have not made such a cover in nearly thirty years, I no longer protect my books, I underline in ink, scrawl into margins in ball-point, immediately break their backs with a crack when I get them home from the store to make them lie flat from the start. I turn down pages, I do every last thing to my books that my Austrian upbringing should make me abhor. *Eselsohren* we were taught to call a dog-ear. A turned-down corner was not merely something that looked like an ear—a dog's or a donkey's—but *Esel* applied to anyone who turned down pages, too: uncouth as an ass.

Lots of *Eselsohren* in my books and no covers to protect them or me, I am stuck with this violence in my room, on my bed, on my dark blue rug. When I am ready to go to sleep I edge under the covers and feebly push at the mountain of books, nudge them to the side a few inches, the blanket of swastikas shares my bed with me.

When I wake up, there it all is again. The monster board with its labels, the scrawled note, *Feb. 6, 1940, Mutti pregnant?* above the clipping, *February 12: First deportation of Jews from Germany, April 9: Invasion of Denmark and Norway, May 10: German invasion of Belgium, the Netherlands, and Luxembourg.* When my mother was four months pregnant with me, *Declaration of war by Italy on Great Britain and France. President Roosevelt calls this a stab in the back.* In her ninth month, *First draft in the United States, 16.4 million men registered,* and *Deportation of Jews from Baden, the Saar, and Alsace-Lorraine. Nov. 6, 1940, me,* has no historic correlative, but pinned next to the date on which my mother was up and around again, nursing me—"You were finicky at first, but then you really took to it"—the snippet says, *Warsaw Ghetto sealed.*

Dominating this particular area on my board is a photograph of my father. He is thirty-five. It is a three-quarter portrait, clear-eyed gaze directed toward distant vistas, black hair cut short at the sides but full above a high forehead, the strong jaw and chin I have inherited looking beautifully proportioned on him, a serious, perfectly shaped, luscious movie-star mouth. He wears a white

64

shirt, and the knot of his dark tie sits a little askew, endearing to me. The photograph ends at the notch of the lapel of a tweed suit. Since insignia seem to have been worn below the notch, this photograph lacks all political identification.

I have a few others of him from around this period, also wearing a suit, decorated with a narrow bar-pin and a doodad that looks like a tiny bell, or possibly a miniature brass instrument. The photographs are small, and I cannot make out the meaning of his decorations, but he is clearly not wearing a swastika pin. There are no photographs of him in uniform, except amid a military band, he is in his early twenties. I puzzle about this. My mother once told me, smilingly, "He had his uniforms tailor-made long before he became an officer, he was vain back then." Not a single photograph of my vain, uniformed father. Did he destroy them all, later? That would explain it. But why would he not have had at least this particular photograph taken in uniform? It is an official portrait, no little snapshot in the park like the others. On its back he wrote in his beautifully flowing, flamboyantly graceful script, "In grateful love to my dear, brave wife in memory of Ingelein's first birthday. Father. Munich, 1941."

There he was, having been sent to Munich by his Nazi cop superiors in order to get a belated high school education; it was 1941, still a time when it seemed as if the war would be won by his side. Life must have smiled on an Austrian Nazi who had been an *Illegaler* for years: a National Socialist long before the *Anschluss* and the attending rush of "March Violets," those hundreds of thousands of Austrians who became Nazis when the time was right.

He had good reasons to have himself photographed in a tailored uniform; it would have been the appropriate garment to wear on a good-size photograph signed "Father," to be sent to his wife back home, commemorating the birth (he had held my mother's hand during the delivery) of his daughter, of whom he was very proud and whom he had named—not Maria, or Theresia, or Veronika,

65

or Ursula, or any other traditional Austrian name—but Ingeborg: "Either the daughter or the mistress of some god called Borg," as someone once explained to me, as Nordic a name as an Austrian can come up with.

I slept with one Jewish man once, with a second one several times,
a man who was "fascinated" by my "background" and liked to
hear, in bed, about my father. I stopped meeting him because I
got scared: Playing with fire/Risking the wrath of . . . whose
wrath? It felt like defiant slumming, exotic and perilous, more
perverse than anything involving the mere manipulation of bodies,
if my father could see his Ingelein now.

According to my bulletin board, August 21, 1944, was the opening day of the *Dumbarton Oaks Conference on the formation of the United Nations*; American newspapers must also have proclaimed, *United States forces advance on Paris*. In Graz that day, nurses and doctors, summoned to the hospital's basement shelter by warning sirens, abandoned my mother on the delivery table. She gave birth to her son alone. He was nine months old and gravely ill with encephalitis on May 8 of the following year, the day the Allies call *V-E Day*. Directly below, my handwritten note on an index card says, *May 9, 1945, Russians take Graz*.

But the Russians soon swapped Graz to the British for other considerations, and there is a photograph of the town hall bedecked with British flags, British tanks out front, and a couple of British sentries. It's just a flag, I tell myself, and some tanks they had no more use for, the war was over.

I have pinned a 1978 postcard next to those English sentries, a postcard of that same town hall lit up for the festivities celebrating the eight hundred and fiftieth birthday of Graz. (In the sixth century, a fortress "gradec"; 1128, name "Graz" recorded for the first time; 1278, passes into possession of Habsburgs; 1379, Friedrich III commissions castle, cathedral, and city gates; 1533 and 1580, Turks burn all villages in the vicinity but are rebuffed by heavily armed city; 1578, Jesuits found university, which becomes focal point of Counter-Reformation; Johannes Kepler teaches here, 1594–1600; Turks defeated once more, 1664; 1738, first opera house; 1797 and 1805, besieged by French; 1809, surrender to French, much of it razed, people of the city pay large sum to save bell and clock tower; 1919, new frontiers place the provincial capital in a border region devoid of the all-important resources of the former Austro-Hungarian Empire; etc.) It was temporary after all, and the British flags don't fly in front of my *Rathaus* anymore. Still, the sight of these alien, crisscrossing stripes hanging from this lovely, boring, run-of-the-mill baroque building at the center of my hometown. . . .

All the statistics I know about my parents are collected here, along with "historical" dates of the period. It's all there now and I wake up each morning with a start and stare at this imposing monster grab-bag, and I still can't keep the dates and facts in my mind together. Something interferes. I cannot see my parents as part of it. Not long enough, at any rate, to make specific, personal data click into place on the grid of official history, not long enough to fit an Ernst Seiler and a Juliane Margarete Vallant Seiler into a *Kristallnacht*—did they watch, that night, Jews' shop windows being smashed, a mob, excitement, a fire here, rumors of a larger one across town? Did Ernst Seiler throw a few rocks himself? Would he have? Wouldn't he have? Am I reduced to a single conviction about my father and that particular night: that he wouldn't have touched so much as a tin spoon, no thief, *Vati*, no looter? "There are only two instances that grant a man the miserable right to steal—and they are these: if his family is about to starve, I mean *starve*; and if the very lives of members of his family are at stake." I remember how he would set his mouth, having once again pronounced one of Seiler's laws, how curious I thought it, at nine, eleven. He could make his lips, always now turned down at the corners, but still full, my father had a beautiful mouth, how he could make his mouth appear thin-lipped, but without seeming to draw his lips in, or not so that I could notice it, there was a period of half a year during which I tried to imitate how he would set his mouth to nearly hide his lips. I used my mother's small, round pocket mirror for my practice sessions. My brother used the same mirror to annoy neighbors by beaming "sunspots," as he called them, onto their windows. So that much I know. He would not have been among the looters. Setting fires doesn't fit either, arson seems out of character for him, it takes so little initial effort, the eventual spectacle, the grandiose, blazing violence all vicarious, done for you. But smashing a large, polished, plate-glass window, bashing in two, four, half a block's worth of Jewish storefronts, a different story, that. Far easier to imagine than having him watch—no, he wouldn't have just watched. He could, of course, have been inside, at home, totally out of the picture. Could he have? As a street cop? Weren't they all rounded up, all out there, on full alert, though not to keep windows from being smashed or a sixty-five-year-old tailor from being knocked sprawling on a sidewalk; the rabble climbing over him to get into his shop, grabbing five men's suits, still on hangers, one of them unfinished, neat white basting-stitches marking what the length of a sleeve was to be, the half centimeter to be taken off at the shoulders, the man carrying the suits is short and breathes heavily through an open mouth, the hangers are getting in the way, annoying, how they knock against his chin, nose. Margarete Juliane surely was at home that night, that's no mere guesswork, no fantasizing now. Just as surely as *he* would not have been among the looters, just as surely he'd have ordered *her* to stay at home, behind locked doors. Might she have huddled in a back room, covering her ears with the palms of her hands, a gesture all her own, that one, some initiative of her own left then, after all? Of course, he might even have *prevented* the smashing of windows, might have kept a small mob at bay, one cop's gun against a handful of men, clerks or assistants to the chef at a good restaurant, *Leberknödelsuppe* a specialty; armed now with a reedy-looking table leg, a hammer, a crowbar. Why would they battle a cop with a gun, if all they had to do was round a corner to find a sergeant who'd watch them go at it, face impassive, or one who'd join them in ransacking a shoe store, a pawnshop, there, grab that silver-plated figurine before the fat guy gets a hold of it, too late, but there are jade bracelets and radios and fur collars next door, the whole-animal-kind, little black claws intact on slender paws, glass eyes. There *were* cops like that, not many, but some. Not necessarily "Jew-lovers," but disciples of order who considered a mob, out for nothing but material gain, contemptible, who managed to save a window from being smashed on one block, a store owner's head from being bashed in by a bentwood hatstand wielded by a sixteen-year-old printer's apprentice. Considering how fervently Ernst Seiler adored discipline and order, could he not have been one of those few, behaving in a manner befitting a human, if only by default? It is as plausible and as possible, as implausible and as impossible, as imagining him hurtling the first, large brick through window after window, moving on after each satisfying crash, letting the others bother with splinters and shards, protecting themselves against little accidental cuts, common, surely, all that frantic shoving, getting your hands on the loot, Jews' loot.

Mere speculation. There was no *Kristallnacht* on farms; whether or not my relatives living on those farms know what my parents, by then living in the city, were up to that night is a moot point. They do not speak about such matters. At most, they allow as how one could not believe that a man like "der Ernstl" could ever have been involved in "anything like that." Not "der Ernstl," who built a house brick by brick, who designed and cut and soldered awkwardly proportioned, clumsy-looking constructions of solid iron tubing meant to hold my mother's ever-expanding collection of houseplants, his Christmas presents to her; the plants obscured the massive iron limbs beneath, and the final effect pleased my mother very much. For us children he made a sled from the same solid iron tubing (webbing from a lawn chair, discarded by one of the English officers, was painstakingly rewoven to serve as the sled's seat), a killer sled. Now I wonder how we were lucky enough never to collide with anyone riding a "regular" wooden one, a luxury, rich kids' gear; my father's soldered iron menace would have reduced those elegant, varnished wooden curves to splinters. It was exhausting, dragging that vehicle home at the end of an afternoon, more exhausting yet pulling it uphill, but coming *down*, ah, no one else's sled could come close to the feel and speed of our homemade, solid-iron wonder. And there was an iron-tubing abacus, too, easily half a yard high. I remember it as well as the sled, I do not need to be reminded by relatives of what all he did for us children, and under such meager circumstances, too. "He loved making things by hand almost as much as he liked his music," one of my mother's friends points out to me, "a man like that does not destroy, willfully, heedlessly, he had no greed in him, your father. *Der Herr* Seiler was a man of honor, how you can even pose such questions, he was a smart man, an outstanding chess player, a musician as versatile as I've known no other, a craftsman who loved working with his hands, *making* things, *installing* windows, not smashing things to bits, I am ashamed of you for your thoughts."

Everything she says is, in its way, correct. I *am* ashamed "for my thoughts," at least for a little while. But the nagging soon resumes, that slight but incessant clawing, that wondering going on inside the tiniest toy bunker, installed, unobtrusively, in a short, narrow alleyway of the right hemisphere of my brain, a fairyland bunker far smaller than any computer crystal dreamed up so far; sitting there, solid, protecting the rest of my cerebral territory from being invaded by whatever it is, clawing and pawing, most often barely at my level of perception, then for hours, days, not to be ignored: *Vati, Vati,* what did you do and why?

So my day has started again and I edge out of bed and remake the corner I've slept in and there is my cat, stretching her torso across *Hitler's War*, one of her back paws planted on *Mein Kampf*, the other one on the spine of *The European Right*, squashing *Varieties of Fascism* and shedding black, silky hair on *The Encyclopedia of the Third Reich*.

I go to the kitchen to make coffee and drink it standing up, my back to my corny, genteel bedroom, ruffled pillows covered with swastika-books, the apartment of a lunatic. "The premises were littered with Fascist literature," it would say in a police report.

A gruesome murder in this city is followed by a trial. There is a
photograph in the *Times*. The caption reads: "Members of the
Hasidic community of Crown Heights gather in a hallway during
recess in Brooklyn trial."

I cut out the photograph because it brought me to a halt while
leafing through the paper, a halt first and then an acceleration of
leafing and then going back to it, and scrutinizing it, and cutting it
out, and now the clipping is turning yellow.

It is a photograph of eight or nine men. Most wear glasses, as I
do, most are smoking freshly lit cigarettes. As a chain smoker, I

can appreciate their relief at being released from a tense, NO SMOKING room into the nearest hallway. All have their heads covered, most by hats, a couple by yarmulkes. There is nothing foreign-looking about a yarmulke to someone brought up as a Roman Catholic. The hats are all the same except for the one on a man in the background whose hat is pulled forward, a "fashionable" hat. All the others are narrow-brimmed and pushed off the forehead. Either they are too small, or the angle at which they are worn makes them appear too small.

The tilt of hats, dark suits, beards. Only one man wears a discernible sidelock: quaint, maybe amusing, not the current fashion in men's hair, but a pretty ornament, really; what would I give to have hair of this texture?

When I try to dissect what I see on this photograph, all I come up with are aesthetics on the most superficial of levels, that of fashion. And I know well that an Austrian *Dirndl* costume can seem odd, that rucksacks are considered quaint by many people in this country, that men in leather shorts and pointed hats with feathers strike most Americans as hilarious.

But my reaction has nothing to do with curls and tilts of hats. There is an emotion in me that cannot be synchronized with any one detail, or with a congregate of these details. It is a quick, short rush, a smell, that taste in your mouth that first warns you that you are going to be sick. It passes before I can become fully conscious or ashamed of it, I let it—make it—pass, quick, quick, over, over. But staring at a crumpled newsprint photograph I find that as fleeting as the sensation is, it does not exhaust itself. I cannot point to a single detail and say, "Here! See? I am offended by such-and-such, I am put off by this-and-the-other." Yet no matter how often I look at the photograph, my reaction persists. I dislike—intensely, specifically—a group of men smoking in a hallway. I don't know these men. I have, in fact, not once in my life spoken to a man in a tilted black hat with a narrow brim, and

76

a sidelock. So what is it? Simply that these men are proclaiming, publicly, through a combination of innocuous details, that they are Jews.

For sixty-eight of his eighty-six years, Franz Josef I spent his days, by the Grace of God, as Emperor of Austria, Apostolic King of Hungary, King of Bohemia, King of Dalmatia and Lodomeria, Duke of the Bukovina, Duke of Upper and Lower Silesia, and Margrave of Moravia.

I don't know how many of history's acknowledged rulers managed to stay on a throne for more than sixty-eight years. There may be scores of them. But I was taught only about one, his persistence in sticking to the business of ruling continues to impress me, and sixty-eight years do add up to seventeen four-year administrations.

At the beginning of this century, one segment of this emperor's subjects consisted of German-speaking Austrians, like those on both sides of my family. Most of them were born in a village, lived there, and were honorably buried within walking distance of where they had spent their lives. They were inhabitants of a mighty empire (whose size they did not comprehend) mainly in terms of what there may exist above and beyond being born, living, and dying.

Various notions of "above and beyond," inextricably linked to the notion of "Mighty Empire," meant a great deal to other Austrians of the time. To a philosopher, for instance, or to a pioneering physician, to a politician of that era, its scholars, composers, would-be revolutionaries, artists, intellectuals, prominent businessmen and poets, or to a lovely, nervous, very young and emerald-laden minor duchess about to attend her first ball at court.

But for Austrians akin to my family, "above and beyond" consisted of loyalty to Franz Josef I, the only ruler in memory of the great majority of his subjects, and a vague pride, inculcated in grammar school, in one's country's "history." Roman Catholicism, and the security that was rooted in belonging to a family, a place, and a craft, were also among an Austrian villager's "above and beyond" categories, but those realms were connected only loosely to being a citizen of the Empire.

Within the Empire, "my kind" of Austrians, along with all other German-speaking inhabitants, were a minority whose status was increasingly in question. The "primitive, endlessly squabbling Slavs"—as Austrians were fond of describing their compatriots to the south and east—were becoming more than a nuisance. "Squabbling Slavs" had, of course, made up the majority of the Austro-Hungarian Empire for centuries. But if Franz Josef I chose to reside in Vienna, to speak German, and to have his far-flung bureaucracy administered by German-speaking Austrians, well, that was a Serb's tough luck.

One such Serb decided to turn luck's tide. He assassinated "our" Crown Prince and managed, through his beastly deed and all by himself, to cause the First World War—or so I was taught in Austrian history classes in the 1950s. In the 1960s, on a visit to Sarajevo, I was shocked to see a bridge and a street named after the assassin; to have a place on the sidewalk, where he might have stood while aiming his pistol, pointed out proudly by local tourist guides; to watch the "assassin" of my history classes turn a corner and reappear a "hero," a "revolutionary," a "saint."

In an American high school in 1979, my daughter seems to be learning the "assassin" version. I have become fond of Gavrilo Princip's wardrobe of mantles; I am glad he lived. When it gets too tiresome to muddle through the complex issues that precipitated that war, simplicity and comfort await me in the fairy tale that Princip caused it all.

For a long time, measured by the passage of centuries, there had existed a vast, many-checkered, multicolored, often glorious piece of fabric crisscrossed with seams, a territory. At times, bloodstained stretches had been concealed by embroidery, possibly stitched so crudely as to perpetuate an original affront from great-grandfather to son; in luckier times a light hand had been at work, using patience, and hair for thread, a gold thimble thrown in for good measure.

To me, the operetta names of those countries sound like an ecclesiastical litany, or like a list of sophisticated foods, the victors' banquet in a restaurant of class. What shall it be . . . L'Autriche à la Russe? Spicy *paprikash* stirred at your table by an authentic Gypsy, a choice morsel of veal called "Bohemian Night Life," many an Englishman's longings fulfilled; a success all around. And now our French guest requires dessert, he pouts, a sweet is called for and here it is: light as air, lacy as spun sugar, lovely Moravia.

This culinary approach—which slice of territory or influence ends up on whose victor's serving platter—is mere fantasy, of course. Fact is, by the end of the First World War, the Austro-Hungarian Empire was snipped into different pieces. The Empire was dead, a group of new nations had been born. "Austria" was one. A major question concerning this new Austria soon became urgent: What is it?

While it proved arduous to come up with an answer, someone did turn up with a name. The new Austria was dubbed a "torso" or, variously, a "rump" nation.

Once, late at night, I tried a variation of counting sheep, enumerating body parts that might have been more closely descriptive of my country's relative new size and shape. But if ventures into gore seem fatuous when all that is called for is a better label, and if one can get used to the idea of an empire as a house instead of a body, then it becomes appropriate to call the new Austria a short, dead-end hallway.

Once the First World War was over, the Allies' two-year blockade kept all food and coal out of the new Austria, that segment of the former monarchy that had depended on the Empire's southern and eastern regions for such necessities; most Austrian farms barely supported the people who lived on them. While the Allies may have seen this blockade as a diplomatic tool (now that the world had been made "safe for democracy," it was time to ensure a lasting peace), Austrians saw it as revenge at its most vicious.

At the same time, all those German-speaking civil servants who had administered the Empire for Franz Josef I came home, along with a stream of former career officers of the Austro-Hungarian army; they received pensions that did not support their families, forcing all of them to look for work and, of course, places to live. Graz was soon dubbed *Pensionopolis*. Simultaneously, an extraordinary number of refugees from the east poured into Austrian cities and tried to make do, twelve to a basement room. Jewish and Christian city dwellers alike went on forays into the countryside, attempting to buy food. But there are no calories in money, and farmers were not willing to sell what they needed to survive. As people in cities became desperate, they stole what food they could find in the fields, sometimes fighting farmers for their lives. Memories of marauders, crazed with hunger and on the rampage, were to fester in the hearts of city and country people alike. The raids benefited few. The poorest—Galician Jews along with Viennese Christians—starved.

Who was there to turn to? Who could help? Who would?

As a newly landlocked country, Austria had seven next-door neighbors. There was Italy to the south, but, in *this* World War, Italy had been one of the Allies. To the south and east were those former family members, exuberant at having watched the Empire croak, reeling with talk of freedom and self-determination. In 1979, their grandchildren are ruled by committees of commissars. I hope they are happier under the commissars than their grandparents were under Franz Josef I, among whose more repressive measures had been an insistence that birth certificates were to be printed in German. (Of course, I would not relish having mine printed in Serbo-Croatian either.)

To the west was Liechtenstein, a lovely country of sixty-two square miles, populated by roughly twenty thousand inhabitants, not a power to rely on in a crisis. Also to the west, next to Liechtenstein and somewhat larger, was a prosperous country unblemished by war and turmoil. "But those Swiss are a joke," as one aging Styrian tells me. "If so much as a baby deer farts near one of their scrawny little borders, they lock up for good. Three people I know, all of them skilled laborers, applied for visas to get in there and work at a time when the Swiss had jobs going wanting. Not one got in. No slot for a hungry neighbor, never a place for a refugee. All the Swiss ever have room for is banks."

He spits vigorously on the ground beneath the park bench on which we both sit. "Well, never mind. When did an Austrian ever have anything in common with a Swiss? They've got higher mountains than we do and they can't even yodel, did you know that?"

I did not.

"They *pretend*," he concludes. "But they never quite bring it off."

That left Germany.

Germans and Austrians had fought and lost on the same side of a disastrous war, and Germany was not to be written off as a ghost; it had suffered overwhelming defeat, but it was, compared to Austria, still vast. "Besides, Germany is like a *Wienerschnitzel*," as one of my relatives explains to me. "The more you beat it, the bigger and better it gets." Austrians implicitly believed in the stereotype of Prussian efficiency and determination; if anyone could manage to rebuild a broken country, Germans would, and a recovered Germany might come to Austria's aid.

For their part, the efficient Germans tended to regard Austrians in terms of those familiar assumptions held about "south-of-the-border" folk anywhere, a set of clichés so pervasive as to be not only hilarious in its repetitiveness but nearly endearing. (What *does* it do to a nation's psyche not to have a southern neighbor? Whom *do* you feel superior to on the South Pole?) To many Germans, Austrians were and are a slovenly lot, shiftless, slow, and lazy by nature. Austrians retaliate with jokes:

Six burly Austrians are trying to dislodge a rock from a path they want to make into a road. Eventually they give up. They are discussing their project, standing in a circle around the rock, when who should come along but two Germans.

Guten Tag! say the Germans, and, *Gibt's hier ein Problem?* The Austrians explain: road, rock. The Germans look at each other, four eyes briefly roll upward, two men approach the rock, each gets a good grip, one of them counts, *eins, zwei, drei,* the rock has been dislodged.

The Austrians sit down on a grassy boulder at the side of the path, get out their lunch, and begin to eat. The Germans, sweaty and triumphant, survey the chomping group. Six of them had not been able to budge a rock!

When none of the Austrians says a word, the Germans get annoyed. "Well?" asks the first. "Nothing?" And the second one adds, "Maybe a quick 'thank you' might suit the occasion?"

Finally an Austrian does speak up. "Force," he says, and shakes his head. "You moved it by force. Any fool can move a rock using *force. . . .*"

But Germany was not merely a neighbor to latch on to in need. If nationalism is pride in one's country—or excessive pride, coupled with indifference, callousness, or hostility toward other countries—Austrian nationalism had a twist of its own. Even before the First World War, the most nationalistic of Austrians had simultaneously been those most fervently Pan-German. As the Empire's German-speaking minority had come to feel increasingly hemmed in by Pan-Slavism, its most nationalistic segment longed ever more ardently to be united with Germany; a nationalism based on language, imbued with passions more primary than any aroused by political boundaries.

"German" was shorthand for an immensely rich culture shared by both nations, a common heritage of literature, music, and philosophy, a joint realm of ideas, one state of mind. To define this state in political terms was, for the time being, out of the question. The Treaty of Versailles expressly forbade a union between Germany and Austria. But there were people in both countries who resolved, and obstinately so, that a unity of heritage and language would, eventually, take precedence over lines on a map.

I have almost finished reading *The Nature of Prejudice* by Gordon Allport. "Not that old thing," exclaims a friend on the phone, and I surmise, accurately, that he had to read it as an undergraduate many years ago. But I had never heard of the book and find it fascinating.

Allport separates prejudice into *attitude* and *beliefs*. The *attitude* is inculcated early, while the *beliefs* are formulated later and serve as "rational" bolsters for the *attitude*.

I study the *beliefs*, amazed. "Jews are clannish," it says, in a list of stereotypes held by American Christians about Jews. "They are grasping and covetous," "money is their god," "they are noisy and cause commotions. . . ." I have to laugh out loud.

I put down the book and try to formulate what beliefs I have about Jews, Jews in general, Jews as a category. "Clannish," "covetous," "money-hungry," and "noisy" don't apply. I concentrate for a while, trying to come up with a stereotype of my own, but to no avail. So I count the Jews I know instead, I consciously sort them, I separate them from the general body of my friends and put them into a special group. No longer Barry and Janie and Judith and David and Henry, Gerry, Wendy, Suzanne, and Fred, but "my Jewish friends." What is there to be said about them? Some are writers or editors, all are smart, otherwise they have nothing in common. Some of my Christian friends happen to be in the same field, they are not dullards either, nor do they have anything else in common. I would be unable to complete the sentence: all my Jewish friends . . . Or this one: all the Christians I know . . .

According to Allport, what I am doing is called refencing. "When a fact cannot fit into a mental field, the exception is acknowledged, but the field is hastily fenced in again. . . . By excluding a few favored cases, the negative rubric is kept intact for all other cases." But this negative rubric is, for me, a category devoid not only of specific people, but unencumbered by a single stereotype. Allport does not allow for that. "Without some generalized beliefs concerning a group as a whole," he says, "a hostile attitude could not long be sustained." That's where Allport is wrong, that's where he severely underrates the power of the irrational.

My father was six when his father died, and eight at the start of the First World War. The last two war years were bad; the family lived on potatoes. Still, they made it through.

By the time the Habsburg Monarchy collapsed, my father was twelve. Having spent the last four of his six years in school absorbing a wartime version of education (which presented to pupils their own country's quest versus its foes' as vividly as wartime propaganda everywhere seems to demand), my father now had two years of peacetime elementary school ahead of him. During those two years his teachers, along with the vast majority of teachers across Austria and Germany, did their utmost to instruct the children in their charge in the necessity for revenge against the enemies in the Great War, in hostility toward anything that might be described as "democratic" (the hated French had "invented" this form of government) and in adulation of everything "German." Teachers also made a point of explaining that evil—and Jewish— politicians at home had sold out the soldiers at the front, thereby causing this utterly implausible defeat of brave Austrian and German troops. This had clearly not been true. However, what proved to be important was not "truth," but that a seamy legend ended up being believed by most Austrians, and that Hitler made competent use of this "stab-in-the-back" theory not too much later.

The two years following the war were harder to endure than the war itself, but my father's mother managed to continue to feed her family: the cow's milk—there was less and less of it because of poor feed—sold in minute amounts; the few chickens' eggs bartered one by one; the potatoes, tended like prize roses, never eaten whole now, but stretched into thinner and thinner soups.

When my father left school, Austria's democracy was two years old, and neither Austria nor democracy was doing well. The First Republic had come about not through popular demand or support, but as the result of military collapse. It had been imposed on Austria by the victors of a war the Austrians had lost. There was no tradition of democracy; most Austrians did not understand how this new system was supposed to work, considered their political parties—unable to come to a consensus on any course of action—useless, blamed their new government for the appalling economic situation, and wanted someone, somehow, to relieve their misery. "There is a general cry for a strong government," says a 1919 police report from socialist Vienna, the one place in Austria where one might not have expected such sentiments, "which would rally all forces to attend to the needs of the people and above all would see to it that the inhabitants of this state have enough to eat and to keep warm." Three-quarters of Vienna's population concurred.

Round about that time, historians tell us, a large part of Austria's conservative, Catholic population felt "threatened." Moreover, specific "subgroups"—what historians call the peasantry, small shopkeepers, and craftsmen or artisans—felt, along with other subgroups, particularly threatened.

It took me a while to figure out who these subgroups were, and that was no historian's fault but mine. Those terms evoked a hazy imagery in my head, combinations of countless movie and advertising clichés. "Peasantry." Doesn't it conjure up thatched roofs, wooden plows, a woman in a long skirt and bits of hay in her hair lacing up her bodice as lusty Tom Jones rides on to new adventures? And ought not a "small shopkeeper" to be someone cozily quaint, a portly man behind a polished counter handing penny-candy to smiling urchins on tiptoes? The "artisan" is surely a Swiss jeweler wearing a gleaming leather apron; he examines gold filigree under an antique magnifying glass, his apple cheeks atwinkle at the prospect of looking up to greet the tourists.

Only when I got past this nonsense and connected sociohistoric-al categories with real people did I realize that they were intimately familiar to me. No one in my family, either on my father's side or on my mother's, did *not* fit into one of these categories. It's simple on my mother's side—peasantry all. But what about my father's mother? She ran a grocery store in a room off her kitchen (offering four bolts of fabric, thread, tablets of paper, shoe polish, and nails, in addition to pickles, flour, sugar, salt, and the like) but also kept that cow and half a dozen chickens and planted and harvested her own small potato field. Combining these occupations with relentless, brain-numbing effort, she had been able to feed, if not adequately clothe, six children (the youngest was two when her husband died) even during the last years of the Great War and those first years following it, when people in cities died of starvation. Was she a "small shopkeeper/peasant" or a "small peasant/shopkeeper"? Whatever her sociologically correct label, she did what countless of her peers in either category were also doing. She fought to stay alive.

When historians point out that large groups of Austrians at that time felt "threatened," they cite a number of factors that might have contributed to such a feeling. What, then, was there to be threatened by?

There was the disappearance of the monarchy, for a start. Gone, vanished. Those Habsburgs into whose possession Graz had passed in 1278—gone. Centuries and centuries, generation after generation after generation of Habsburgs—vanished. Replaced by whom? No one was too sure. But whatever the replacement consisted of, it offered no protection, it was of no help. Or how about this one: an order, in which all had known their place—no more. An unshakable framework, a cohesive world, not always a pleasant one, often fraught with injustice and hardship, but a world one could depend on, a world that changed very slowly and remained, even in change, secure—gone. Age-old tradition and all that—no more. Now the Bolsheviks were trying to start a Soviet Republic in Austria, Communists and Socialists alike wanted one group of Austrians to fight other groups of Austrians under the banner of something called "class war," the Social Democrats already ruled Red Vienna. And finally all the rest, all those factors that were not merely disorienting. All those men who had come back, bitter and defeated, from a World War they had lost, the "first total war in history," all those men who had come back wounded, all those who had not come home at all. The near-starvation of the last war years and the years after the collapse, the continuing scarcity of food, of coal, of living accommodations, of jobs, life savings melting in the inflation and no improvement in sight. One's helplessness in the face of it all.

It seems to me that historians, when they enumerate the factors that might have contributed to this "threatened" feeling, sometimes fail to make clear that people were not "threatened by inflation" one day, "feared a Bolshevik takeover" a month later, or worried about "a scarcity of food and coal" every other Tuesday. A reader finds out about such factors one at a time, consecutively. But to the people involved, whose lives had been drastically changed for the worse, these were not separate, alternate, or even consecutive "factors." They were calamities, and people were overwhelmed by all of them, and at the same time.

It's enough to put someone in shock. Of course, none of the peasants or small shopkeepers or artisans I know suddenly wandered aimlessly into the nearest field, unseeing eyes fixed on the horizon. People carried on. They worked harder than ever, made do, and lived—as one does in any dreadful, interim, emergency situation—one day at a time. But I would be surprised if a great many Austrians of that period were not—collectively—in a state of shock.

Beginning in 1920, once the Allies lifted their postwar blockade, food and coal became available again. Unfortunately, the mere ·availability of food did not mean that everyone was able to afford it.

"Between the ages of fourteen and seventeen my father nearly starved" is a tempting phrase but would not apply, since he was, once again, not threatened by starvation as such. "Continually hungry" wouldn't be quite right either. For three years, between 1920 and 1923, two or three times a month, my grandmother traveled by train, third class, from Burgau (her village in the province of Styria) to Mödling (a small town near Vienna in the province of Lower Austria) to bring her son food. I assume that my father was able to eat until he was full on those occasions, and that he had enough food left over to last him another couple of days. Between the ages of fourteen and seventeen then, my father, who was a slight and wiry boy, grew by a number of centimeters and lost a number of kilograms. I wish I knew both numbers, but I don't.

Mödling was where my grandmother had found an apprenticeship for her son Ernst. An apprenticeship, like education of any kind after the elementary grades, cost money. My grandmother could not afford to pay for three years' worth of Ernst's apprenticeship, not with the younger children still at home, not after already having paid for apprenticeships for the two older boys. But she asked all the people she knew to ask everyone they knew if anyone had heard of a "free" apprenticeship. A tradesman who needed but could not afford another worker would sometimes take on an apprentice instead. It was understood that such a freeloading apprentice would work especially hard.

Someone did hear of a free post, though situated farther away than expected. My grandmother took some cotton out of her store, a neighbor sewed two new shirts for my father, and at the age of fourteen he left for Mödling to become a locksmith.

He was unhappy at the thought of entering this particular trade. But his mother encouraged him to take pride in the fact that—through a fluke, without even trying—he was going to learn the same trade that his father and grandfather had learned, an honorable trade. She also reminded him that the trade a boy like him might learn was not a matter of choice. His older brother Eduard had become a baker because there had been an inexpensive apprenticeship available in a local bakery. It was important only that a boy learned some trade, any trade, since a man without a trade was destined to be a hired hand for life. There was no catching up later.

What had not been made clear by the locksmith in Mödling was this: while he would not ask for the customary fee, and while he desperately needed an extra man for his shop because he had a bad back, that shop barely supported him and his family. There was not enough money to feed yet one more body.

My father was given coffee before work, again during the midmorning break, and soup at noon and at night. He worked twelve hours a day, slept on a bench in the workshop, was allowed a day off at Christmas and Easter, and lived for those Sundays when his mother would bring him hardboiled eggs and homemade potato strudel. At the end of three years he was a journeyman locksmith.

It was 1923. In faraway Germany, a thirty-four-year-old Adolf Hitler attempted a *Putsch* and was brought to trial. Nearer to home, inflation had reached its peak, there was widespread unemployment and the constant threat of civil war. The Social Democrats had recently organized their own paramilitary organization, the *Schutzbund* (protection corps), in order to combat the *Heimwehr* (home defense). In Vienna, *Heimwehr* units had been organized to put down the Communist revolution. In Styria, farmers and former soldiers had banded together to fight Yugoslav units advancing across the border immediately after the war. Once the Yugoslavs had been rebuffed, the *Heimwehr* continued to parade and prepare. Now that the Social Democrats had their own units, clashes were inevitable. These were not street fights occurring in isolated cities but battles between groups of armed men, and they occurred all over the country, again and again, in the largest cities as well as the smallest villages, straight through the 1920s.

But in 1923, uppermost in my now-seventeen-year-old father's mind was finding a job. He looked first in his own village, then in nearby villages, then in villages farther away. There were no locksmith jobs to be had. Numerous former soldiers, back from the war five years, were still unemployed, work was hard to find. Since it was intolerable for a boy his age to live at home without contributing to the family, since it was difficult enough for his mother to support herself and the girls and the youngest boy, Ernst was soon ready to take any job, anywhere. Besides, whatever he might do would not be for long. Eduard was going to America— where people owned cars and made money they did not need to spend on food alone—and he had promised to send for him soon.

He felt lucky, therefore, when he eventually found work in a coal mine. It meant moving into a boardinghouse, but this time he was, if nowhere near home, at least within his own province. The work consisted of loading chunks of rock, which had previously been blasted from the mountain, onto a cart, pushing the cart along a stretch of tracks, unloading it, and pushing it back again, empty. There were four workers to a cart. For each heaped cart, unloaded at the far end of the tracks, a foreman noted a point for that particular group. At the end of the week each man received, for each cart produced by the team, one fourth of a set amount of money.

If these groups of four worked together smoothly; if they ran instead of walked on their way back with the empty cart; if, above all, they worked without stopping, they could fill and empty enough carts to earn a subsistence wage.

The three men with whom my father was assigned were experienced laborers with large families to support. My father had been undernourished when he began his apprenticeship and was more so now. He couldn't lift half the rocks. If he did manage to lift one, he couldn't carry it to the cart. If he could get some to the cart, he had trouble pushing his corner.

On the second day he fainted. On the fourth, his colleagues beat him up. He came back the next morning. On the tenth day they beat him up again. This time he stayed in bed for two days before going back to work. Two weeks later he fainted again. The day after that he stumbled and fell on the tracks, ten or so yards away from the cart, and an infuriated co-worker strained to push the cart toward him. A second one saw what the first was doing, dropped his rock, and came to the first one's aid.

97

My father managed to roll off the tracks in time to avoid the cart barreling toward him. He crawled a few paces on all fours, got up on his feet, ran all the way to the lodging house, collected his clothes, walked to the nearest village large enough to have a recruiting center, lied about his age, and enlisted in the army. He was a few months short of eighteen.

"Our mother cried and cried," says my Aunt Pepi, my father's younger sister. "The army had a very bad reputation back then. Here he'd stuck it out through those hard years in Mödling, and then he ups and does *that*."

When they were done with all the routine questions, the sergeant asked Ernst Seiler if he played an instrument. He played the violin, as a matter of fact, though that was of little interest to the sergeant. But thanks to a grade-school teacher who had encouraged Ernst, he also played the trumpet, trombone, French horn and tuba, and could get away with a tune on a clarinet as well. They put him into the music division of the 9. *Alpenjägerregiment.*

The army gave him enough money to enable him to send a small amount home every month, which thrilled him out of proportion to the help it could possibly have been to his mother. He did not need to run for his life, no one begrudged him his bowl of goulash. Moreover, what had been a useless hobby at home, involving borrowed instruments, ungainly noise, and time taken away from work, now brought him instant recognition.

As a boy, he had been in no way remarkable for strength, or school grades, or cleanliness, or eagerness to do more than whatever he couldn't get away without. He had been, though surely loved, one of six children his mother supported under nearly insurmountable difficulties.

Now his accomplishments were valued. Not only could he hold his own with the instrument assigned to him, but he could be switched around, he could take other musicians' places if they were sick or on leave. And he wasn't in the band merely in order to avoid a regular unit. He was grateful to be out of the coal mine, he was happy not to have to be a locksmith, he loved playing the marches and polkas and occasional waltzes, he had an infectious laugh and a good time, he made friends.

My father stayed in the army for five years. At some point during that time, between the ages of not-quite-eighteen and twenty-three, he became a National Socialist.

A friend gives me a record: "The Blue Danube," "The Emperor Waltz," overtures to *The Gypsy Baron* and *Fledermaus*, standard father & sons, Johanns and Josef stuff, conducted by Austria's temperamental national treasure, the very von Karajan. Coincidentally, a different friend has presented me with a set of earphones. The story behind the need for earphones is dreary, its villain my upstairs neighbor who claimed that the bass from my stereo made life unbearable for him. Because I respect full-fledged passion, I have been keeping his plight in mind ever since he swung an industrial broom from his window above, three feet of wood beam crashing into my newly washed windowpane.

It's Monday morning, drizzling, dismal, and I decide to put off work for another half hour: I'll try out the Strauss family and my earphones at the same time. I grimace at the sentimental cover, the hyperbolic jacket copy, at myself, and (along with the appropriate twinge of guilt over my ingratitude) at my friend for giving his Austrian friend a record of Austrian waltzes.

"The Blue Danube" laps into motion, civilized and sedate on the perpetual #2 on my Richter scale of volume possibilities. Da, *da*, da, da, *da*, DADA, DADA . . . nice. So familiar as to be ritualized—gelatinized—out of hearing. I listen for another minute before it occurs to me: here's your chance. I make a second cup of coffee, sit down at my desk, put the earphones back on, start the record over. This time I turn the volume knob to six.

An hour later I put away the earphones and the record. It's the noise, I tell myself, anything played this loud—Bulgarian workers' songs, Gregorian chants—will make you cry, one's eardrums pleading with one's eyes to protest the eardrums' demise. Amazing though, there must be a dozen-odd melodies in every one of those waltzes, each enough for a current hit song. Learning to waltz in dancing class—Mirkowitsch, the dancing school considered most appropriate by my classmates' parents. Mine had never heard of Mr. Mirkowitsch but allowed me to attend; I had saved my allowance for nearly a year. Once a week my mother sat on a narrow chair pushed against the wall alongside the other girls' mothers, knitting. Mr. Mirkowitsch himself interrupting a begin-ners' waltz attempted by an anxious, Adam's-apple-bobbing seventeen-year-old and me, an equally anxious sixteen-year-old. No, No, No, Mr. Mirkowitsch booms, and sweeps me away, his mighty belly a priceless aid to my ability to dance, a solid half-globe hollowing out my front from rib cage to pelvis, a misstep made, if not impossible, so surely inconsequential. Propelled by Mirkowitsch's paunch I dance my first waltz, spinning, how light-footed this man was, dancing nightly at the age of sixty-five.

Coming home thrilled, flushed, to find my father asleep at the kitchen table, his head on his arms folded across the day's paper. Waking him up and telling him of my triumph and watching him rub his eyes and grin while my mother takes off her coat and lays her knitting on the kitchen table. "Well, then," he says finally, "let's see if it's true," and shakes off his slippers and bows from the waist and opens the kitchen door to the hallway, and bows again. And then he in his socks and plaid flannel shirt and old gray trousers held up with suspenders, and I in my navy blue dancing-school dress, its white lace collar rumpled, we dance the length of the hallway and back down again past the open kitchen door where my mother stands, the kitchen light behind her, my father and I more deeply in the dark the farther away from her we dance. Down to the front door, straight up again past the kitchen door to where the hallway bends at a right angle, back down the length of the narrow hallway to the front door, my father a better dancer than Mr. Mirkowitsch, and without any paunch at all. I find myself leaning into his arm wrapped around me and into his hand big and warm at the small of my back, and somehow I have finally caught on, after two weeks of fruitlessly counting steps, I have caught on, finally, to that trick of swinging into the next turn before the present one is quite over, tight, glorious whirls. My father singing "The Blue Danube," breaking into a different set of nonsense syllables for each musical phrase, reaching the high notes by cleverly changing pitch in advance, between segments, without missing a single transition and without getting out of breath. He knew the waltz by heart, to the very end.

At the time my father joined the army, my mother left school to tend pigs. ". . . always liked school, but she hired herself out as a *Saudirn* at the age of twelve," said my Aunt Zenzi last summer, when I visited the Styrian mountain farm that turned out not to be my grandparents' farm at all, or not the way I had always assumed it to be: the place where my mother grew up with her parents, those two old people I had called Grandfather and Grandmother. The woman was my grandmother, but she had not raised my mother. "Grandfather" had not been related to me at all.

My mother, it turned out, had been brought up in a small

mountain village just across the border, in Carinthia. Her mother had given birth as an adolescent, the father had not been eighteen. Because of that boy—my real grandfather—the orderly chart I try to construct turns from an ample pine into a banyan tree. Illegitimate children sprout in all directions, each born by a different woman, followed, eventually, by a number of legitimate ones; all of them, irrespective of status under the law, are blessed with numerous offspring. . . . I finally give up on the chart.

My grandmother, as was customary for pregnant adolescent farm girls, turned to the branch of the family that seemed, if not amiably disposed toward, at least able to take care of an additional child. In her case this meant an older, married brother.

When I saw him last summer in Carinthia he wore a dark green hat, an old gray jacket with dark green piping and collar, its buttons made of deer antlers. He held on to a gnarled stick and smoked a pipe, sitting on a weathered bench under a tree, the Picturesque Austrian Mountain Farmer out of a movie.

In his memory, all is well. There had been his own children, of course, ". . . but she was my sister's daughter, you stick together, you take care of your own."

Still, my mother, who had "always liked school," began to earn her keep at the age of twelve. On the lowest rung of any farm's hired-hand hierarchy, reserved for half-witted women and very young, homeless girls, she fed pigs and cleaned out their sties. Zenzi, her youngest half sister, told me so, while we sat at her large, handmade kitchen table in the Styrian mountain farm I remember well from my childhood—the farm I thought my mother grew up on, my grandparents' farm—none of it true. Zenzi was my mother's favorite relative and has been "Aunt Zenzi" to me for as long as I can remember, the woman who had been kind to me when I stayed on the farm as a young child during the war. But my mother did not have any brothers or sisters, not in the strict sense, though there were half sisters and half brothers too numerous to meet. When we go to make a call from the one house in the area that has a telephone, one of my half uncles points out various farms. "That one belongs to an uncle of yours, I mean half uncle, here lives another aunt." He draws my attention to a woman about to walk through the front door of yet another farmhouse, she is bent forward and wears a kerchief. "That one, too, is one of your mother's half sisters." I consider taking yet another snapshot of a relative I have never heard of, then abandon the thought.

There were few abortions among rural Catholics, no adoptions, and numerous illegitimate children. While disapproved of, they were also taken for granted and absorbed, somehow, somewhere, within the confines of large families. My mother's family did not cut people off, no Uncle Eduard among them, no one officially cast out. Her family practiced a different kind of cutting-off. For them, the Austrian farmer's precept, *die Toten ruhen zu lassen*, "to let the dead rest," applied not only to the dead but also to yesterday, and the day before yesterday, and to five years ago or ten. The past deserved its rest too.

According to this well-established system, my mother was bound to be taken in by a member of the family, and so she was. But this self-contained system had its cracks. The idyllic memories of my great-uncle skirt large gaps. He remembers only that she went to school, "like all the other children." The school officials to whom I write to obtain my mother's records do not respond. But back across the border in the province of Styria, in the house I thought was my grandparents' house, my half aunt Zenzi says, "It wasn't easy for her there. She hired herself out as a *Saudirn* at the age of twelve."

Only a few years earlier my adolescent father had slept on a bench in his master's shop. Where did she sleep? I remember the straw sacks in the attic corners allotted to the farm's hired hands. My grandmother had married the man I called Grandfather, but she had not reclaimed her daughter. That one slept on someone's straw sack somewhere, and she received meals. At fourteen she ran away. Or rather, "she went to Vienna." The railroad fare must have been unattainable to a girl who worked for room and board. Did relatives give her the money grudgingly, or readily enough, content to have her leave?

Fourteen, fifteen. I picture my sixteen-year-old daughter on her own, in my mother's shoes, I picture myself. At sixteen, about to exchange continents, I was protected enough not to have been on a date or out of the house by myself after dark.

The worst I can conjure up about her stay in Vienna may be beside the point or may not come close to what happened during those years, which she hid, certainly from her children, probably from her husband, possibly from herself. The twelve-year-old *Saudirn* turned fourteen-year-old maid had metamorphosed, under her own power, into a proper housewife, careful about where she bought meat, knowledgeable over whose greengrocer's onions were cheapest, which bakery had the freshest rolls.

In our house she deferred to my father. *My father,* that's where my mother starts. With him begins her life, as if Ernst Seiler had given birth to her. Instead of stories about her childhood, she would offer the description of how she had met her husband in a movie theater, his gesture of giving her a handkerchief and her description of his smile and the lovely manner in which he had held her elbow and steered her through the crowd once the film was over. The saga of how my parents met is embedded in my memory side by side with the Hail Mary she taught me, I was able to recite both at an early age. Not once did she talk about her adolescence, she only recalled how he proposed to her, during a late spring outing on the *Schlossberg*, the hill in the center of Graz, complete with a list of which trees were in bloom, she was fond of telling this tale and I loved hearing it. She cut herself loose from her past and set it adrift more thoroughly, more completely, with more decisive finality and a far more relentless surface equanimity than my father would be able to muster in cutting loose from his own, some years later, or her daughter a few decades hence. "She always liked school, but she . . ." "She went to Vienna as a young girl." How young? "Oh, fourteen, maybe fifteen." What did she do in Vienna? "I believe she was a maid, we don't really know. Maybe she watched children?" Not even the traditional, quasi-heroic term "runaway" applies, they let her go, it wasn't an issue. At twenty-five, in Graz now, she meets my father. At twenty-six she marries him.

"Everyone was registered, that was the law," a woman at the Austrian consulate tells me. "Anyone changing addresses had to register anew. A branch of the police kept those files. Write to the police archives in Vienna, if she was there they've got to have a record of her somewhere." I do, but there is no record of Juliane Margarete Vallant anywhere. "Well," says the woman at the consulate, "of course there were always people who chose *not* to register, though that was illegal. Fugitives and such." And if she wasn't a fugitive, or not in the sense of the law? "She could always have used a false name. In that case, there isn't a thing you can do about tracing her."

When my mother reappears, it is on the marriage certificate and in my father's records, kept by the police archives in Graz. The woman he marries is described as being Roman Catholic and working in a dairy store. There is no record of when she left Vienna, how long she has been in Graz, or where she lived before her marriage. To wonder about "whys" seems, in the absence of conventional data, nearly presumptuous.

The streetcars in Graz run on tight schedules. In the morning I had to get the 7:17 to be at my desk before the bell rang at 8:00. The 7:27 meant I was late. At the end of the school day my mother knew to the minute when to expect me. The last stop, where the streetcar turns a loop before heading back into town, was two blocks from our house. From our kitchen window my mother could see me climb off, that's when she turned on the burner under the soup she had made for my lunch. Sometimes a teacher would keep us two or three minutes after the final bell. Other times I would buy a candy bar in a shop near the school, which might or might not make me miss a streetcar, and which annoyed my mother since she thought it spoiled my appetite. Four or five times during my high school career I was asked to have lunch at the house of classmates, occasions that filled my mother with a mixture of excitement and dread as she anxiously rehearsed my table manners. She and I were equally aware of the differences between these doctors' or lawyers' families and our own, and the muddled upheaval and pride such invitations aroused in her intimidated, enraged, and pleased me.

Once, when I was sixteen and in dancing school, a boy I had met there waited for me after school, across the street, according to prevailing ritual. Together we slowly walked for a few blocks. It wasn't the boy who excited me, but the idea of him. What my friends were beginning to take for granted, what was the prerequisite for peer esteem in an all-girl school, was finally happening to me, a boy had picked me up after school—a public announcement, an affidavit, proof of desirability.

We shook hands, two stops down the line, and he waved to me once and stood looking after the streetcar until it turned a corner.

Except for my luncheon invitations—always discussed nearly a week in advance—I had never, in nearly six years at the *Gymnasium*, missed two streetcars coming home. I was twenty minutes late, to the second. My mother screamed, most of her words unintelligible except for *Hure, Hure,* whore. She hit me, she screamed even more loudly, she slapped me again, she sank into a kitchen chair with her head buried in her hands, she jumped up repeatedly to slap me some more, finally collapsing in her chair for a last time, sobbing helplessly, desolate. It was the reaction to a catastrophe.

Except for that time, five years earlier, when I had accepted a stick of gum from an English soldier, my mother had not laid a hand on me. *Other* mothers beat their children, I had seen enough kids with bruises in elementary school. But *my* mother did not scream, *my* mother did not hit. She might nag, she might scold, she might cry over a trifle in the newspaper, but those seemed minor quirks in a woman who was, so it appeared to me, balanced, at rest. Not satisfied, there was little to be satisfied with for years, but willing to put up with whatever came along, as cheerful as any woman could be next to a husband who was, for years, granite.

What did not occur to me then—ducking blows, confused, and frightened—I wonder about now, so belatedly, finding myself unable to fill an eleven-year hiatus in my mother's life with even minimal tidbits. What did she imagine was imminent after two missed streetcars, what made her so afraid for me, what did she see while she buried her face in her hands? I tried to leave the kitchen but she would not permit that. I stood with my back against the closed kitchen door, watching her sob. In the end she reached for one of my father's handkerchiefs, which she had ironed only a little while earlier. The old blanket with which she covered the kitchen table while ironing had only been folded, not put away, an alarming sign in itself. The table, though, was set for me to eat.

She blew her nose and wiped her face and then ladled out my soup. My face still hot from the last slap, I ate every drop of the clear, fragrantly seasoned broth, small tender dumplings, freshly cut chives sprinkled on top. Then there was reheated goulash. I sopped up the last drops of gravy with pieces of bread, aware of my mother standing behind me, leaning against the stove, looking at my back.

Neither she nor I said anything to my father or brother about the incident and it did not repeat itself.

As vague as much of my father's life remains to me, I am able to mull over a number of signposts. There are the boyhood stories he told: a railroad going over a bridge, not far above a brook, small boys betting who would dare to crawl up under the bridge and stay there, holding on to the wood beams while the train barreled above his head. My father's grin when he said, "They all fell in, they all let go. It felt like the final judgment, but I held on. I wet my pants and got hell from our mother, but for one day that summer I was a hero." And the cabinets full of files in the Graz police archives, which continue to be tended to whether the men circumscribed in those files have been with the police for the last thirty-odd years or not. And the Berlin Document Center, maintained by the U.S. State Department. Its vast complex of records includes my father's membership card issued by the National Socialist German Workers Party. A photocopy arrives by airmail, the return address is *The United States of America, Official Business*. The cover letter points out that the enclosed is being forwarded "free of cost" and that it is a copy of the only record on Ernst Seiler, indicating that he officially joined the Nazis in Graz, on April 1, 1933, membership number 1,619,667.

How amazing, I think, after the excitement at receiving such an efficient and decisive answer has waned, how amazing. Picture them all, the secretaries who keep those files straight, the officials, the clerks, the person who received and sorted my letter, the one who read it and told someone to look up *Seiler, Ernst*, the clerk who found and photocopied and refiled the card, and whoever dictated and finally typed that letter. And *Seiler, Ernst* was a speck, unknown among party hierarchy. Yet though he was a Nazi nobody, and though he has been dead since 1973, his record is maintained by our State Department. . . .

But thinking about my mother is like stepping onto quicksand or reaching into fog. Nothing is as it appeared, what I assume I know about her turns out to be wrong, she slips through my fingers again and again. In the meantime my eyes begin to burn, I am cold, I am uncomfortably hot, I want to do anything, be occupied with anything else. As if she is saying from the grave: All my life I didn't talk about myself, there will be none of this now that I'm dead, leave me be.

Thanks to my parents' genes I am five foot eight, fair-skinned, and nearsighted. My nose slants toward one side and I have good teeth and a prominent jaw, family characteristics all. Also thanks to my parents' genes and/or example and encouragement I can be charming, do well with languages, and tend to make rash decisions.

When it first dawned on me—this persistent undercurrent, this aversion to things Jewish; for no reason I could pinpoint, and though I fought it as fiercely as I could—I tried to keep my parents out of it. After all, they had never *taught* me a thing about Jews.

Not by example, not in words, nor, so far as I can dredge up, in any realm outside the verbal either. Besides, I told myself, there are a great many things you acquired on your own: a preference for well-worn clothes over new ones, a dislike of Baked Alaska, science fiction, and most sports, a passion for the shade of blue that is furthest away from turquoise. . . .

It is appalling to talk in terms of taste. Much as I try, though, I cannot come up with better comparisons. My convictions are firm: it is evil—and stupid—to be a bigot. "Taste" is the appropriate category. Not just preference but something palpable, something in my mouth.

A characteristic I acquired later then, outside my parents' sphere of influence? Except that this seems so very unlikely. I did not consciously meet a single Jew during the decade I spent in the Midwest. Yet as soon as I started working in New York the instinct—the feeling? the sentiment? the reaction?—was there, as much a part of me as straight hair.

Most of my adult life I have camouflaged my straight hair by getting permanents. Sometimes, when I wait too long, my real hair shows; it not only looks different from the rest, it is impervious to being wound on a curler. Only when the new growth has been altered chemically can I hope to end up with curly hair.

"Hair is composed mainly of protein keratin . . . whether . . . straight or curly depends on the tertiary structure of the keratin molecule," says my encyclopedia. Since "the third month of fetal life" there have been, right below my scalp, nearly two million bulbous roots, programmed to produce straight hair. Until this body is dead, my hair will continue to come out of my scalp straight, no matter how soon and how often I disguise its true state. Unlike my straight hair, my most private of aversions never shows. But it seems equally a preordained matter, the essence of which I have no control over, though I am adept at disguising it; something unvoiced, but part of me nonetheless.

Though that is how it feels—preordained, immutable—it seems

too farfetched to imagine anti-Semitism a matter of genetic property, encoded along with straight teeth or straight hair. Nor does it seem probable that I just caught it, from the air in Graz or a nearby mountain farm. It is also unlikely that a precocious fellow toddler let me in on the ground rules of racism; I had no playmates until the age of five, and by that time Jews were no longer mentioned by anyone I knew.

Even if I don't know when or how, I have no choice but to assume that my parents made clear, somehow, very early on in my life, that they were anti-Semites. I was not born like this, it was done to me.

Sometime before the end of the war, sometime before my brother was born, sometime before my new set of parents came to stay, sometime before it was over . . . there I am, snuggled down in the sidecar of my father's motorcycle. My mother sits behind him, her arms are wrapped around his waist. We travel at angels' speed, trees whiz past and turn into ribbons at either side of the road, snatches of my mother's laughter flit above the engine's roar. Sometimes my father looks back and down at me. His teeth shine, I feel myself shine, a shiny, glistening thrill as the wind howls, as the ribbon of trees unfolds before us, a thrill until now exclusively their own today embraces me.

Some of my mother's hair comes loose from under her scarf and snaps in the wind. Earlier she has squeezed into a pair of my father's trousers, a motorcycle like his is not meant to be mounted decorously, sidesaddle-fashion. The trousers are tight on her, my father had smiled and cupped her behind in both hands, her thigh at my right—I can reach out my hand and touch it—is outlined so as to appear naked; midway through the ride a seam begins to unravel, I watch the sliver lengthen, a sliver of my mother's flesh gleams beside me. The heady reek of gasoline, the leather seat beneath me as pungent as my father's boots, sweet, just-mowed hay, the spice of pines slices through me, fairy-tale sabers.

These two people of splendor belong to me, I belong to them. I am party to their revelry. Her full breasts are flattened against his back, she stretches an arm toward me and squeezes my hand, her face is flushed and dazed above me. This speed, unencountered in dreams, this keen passion, this thrill—I could not bear them were it not for the snug cave that envelops me, wrapped as I am in the blanket from my crib at home, protected by the metal sides of a dream crib bound to the glittery monster that roars under my father's hands. My very own windshield before me, snug as no crib can ever be. Because *this* crib is connected to him and her, they will not abandon the side of *this* crib, not as long as the monster continues to roar. I am tucked in safe, as if in preparation for sleep. But I do not sleep, I gulp instead, I slurp and gobble, I am robbed of breath and drown in wanton angels' speed, a searing sky turns to balm over our self-made storm. I close my eyes and sit up straight and stretch my neck. The storm blasts my forehead, spits grit at my teeth, I swallow it greedily, I lick my lips for more, I know I can always inch down again into my crib and bid the storm vanish at will, off my forehead and nose and mouth, though it roars, even now, in a forgotten part of my brain.

I got my start on anti-Semitism before I had any words. When I was ready to learn the words to go with the feeling, which had already been implanted, none was supplied. "Jews are clannish" means nothing to me. None of the *beliefs* is there to buttress the *attitude*, but that does not faze the *attitude*.

All my adult life I have lived in America, speaking English. In English I merely have a slight pronunciation problem with the word "Jew." I have no trouble pronouncing it in German. But in German, that word never became an "adult" word for me, as it did for my friends back home. At least—even if their parents were like mine and did not speak about Jews; and even though none of us learned anything about Jews in school—they have since had a couple of decades of life in Austria, where a Jew is now chancellor, where Jews are in the headlines and discussed in articles and books. But because I was still an adolescent when I came here to live and to speak only English, the German word—not spoken in Austria while I lived there—has never become a regular word for me, a normal word, just another noun among the hundreds of nouns that are part of my German vocabulary. There has been no adult use, no adult modification. So it has remained raw, attached only to a feeling, a "bad magic" word. *Jude.* It means contemptible, it describes revulsion.

I have been aware of all of this for years now, unable to rid myself of it despite a well-working brain and willpower nurtured by a father who placed great value on willpower. There is, of course, the philosophy that holds that sanity and comfort consist of accepting oneself, faults and all. Does prejudice fall into a category of such faults, something like: right or wrong, my body/mind/anti-Semitism? Do I say to myself: Well, Ingeborg, it seems you are prejudiced. But as long as you don't knock a diamond dealer's hat off with your purse, what's the harm in it? Accept, accept.

If I were a woman from Passaic, New Jersey, whose father had put in a couple of years in the Pacific during the Second World War, whose mother belonged to a volunteer group giving directions and delivering flowers in a hospital, and whose great-grandparents had come to New Jersey from, let's say, Wales; if I were *that* woman and anti-Semitic, I might not go on about it. As it is, I hopelessly love two people who belonged to that party, that movement, that sightless, soulless Moloch that ingested the Six Million. And while it flatters me when a friend looks at photographs of my parents and tells me I smile like my mother or have my father's eyes, I also clench my fists and take quick, shallow breaths in the middle of the night at the thought: How can you go on insisting that your parents could never have had anything to do with . . . with *that?* Why, after all, not? If *you* are uncomfortable looking at a photograph of men you've never set eyes on—and no one ever encouraged *you,* and—wretched, despicable cliché be damned—*some of your best friends are, in fact, Jews?* While they most surely did not know a single Jew personally; while everyone around them took anti-Semitism for granted like rain in April; while prejudice of one form or another against Jews had existed in their country for centuries; while the manifestations of this prejudice had severely escalated within their parents' lifetime. And then there he was, their own, great, beloved leader, who understood an all-pervasive fear and decriminalized the hatred that accompanied this fear, made it official; presented publicly what had long been fantasized privately, and within a context of self-preservation. *Let's get them out!* No talk of killing, mind you, just get 'em out, let somebody else bother with them for a change, they've been enough trouble here, let's get those Jews out of Austria, out of Greater Germany, out, out. . . . Well?

If I try to put myself into my parents' shoes I go down a dizzying spiral and all thought stops. I am just so grateful not to be in their shoes. And I long to be rid of every trace of this creeping sickness that assaults me unawares, over a newspaper photograph, or a researcher's question conjuring up Yiddish. I do not want to accept it, I want it rooted out.

I have two photographs taken of my father while he was in the army. In the first he is nineteen and home on leave. "He saw a picture in the photographer's window," says Aunt Pepi, "and he decided, right there on the spot, that he had to have one just like it."

He looks out at me dreamily, his beautiful mouth not yet set, still vulnerable; one hand in a pocket, a little self-conscious. He has gained whatever weight he needed to gain, he looks as if he has lived through the smoothest of childhoods, he is strikingly handsome in a white shirt with a stiff, stand-up collar, a silk tie, dark coat and vest, pin-striped trousers.

"Where did he get these gorgeous clothes?"

Pepi laughs. "All borrowed. It took him a while to get the pieces together, what a hubbub, he was so determined to look good."

My nineteen-year-old father in a borrowed suit, his perseverance and musical talent all his own. The talent he passed on to his son. For himself, it came to no more than playing the violin some evenings in the basement of "Seiler's Bunker," during the couple of years before he died. I stare and stare at my vulnerable nineteen-year-old father, as if—had I only sufficient insight, patience, wisdom—I could make him tell me what made him happy, what he feared and hoped for. At his age I had undergone the best schooling Austria offers its adolescents, I had been abroad, I was marrying a foreigner; I was full of earnest intentions of being a good wife, dreamed of raising a large family, and took it for granted that I would, once married, miraculously stop biting my nails. What similarities are there to be found between myself at nineteen and my country-hick father of the same age, the boy who had made locks twelve hours a day, had rolled off a set of tracks in time, and, carrying his belongings under one arm, had run to enlist in an army despised by his family? No similarity at all. Except that, at nineteen, what I wanted above all else was an extreme, unequivocal change, a radical break, a new start. He may well have longed for the essence of what drove me.

But I am speculating. The facts I know consist mainly of certain dates and initials: he played in a military band until March 30, 1930; March 31, 1930, was his first day in a different band, that of the Graz police, whose conductor had heard about him through an army buddy; and at some point he joined a group called NSR.

I first heard about this organization through a polite reply to various queries I had addressed to the Graz police archives. The letter relates, in formal officialese, that Ernst Seiler was dismissed from the police force in 1945 because of his membership in the NSDAP, his membership in the SS, and his membership in the NSR. "SS" is clear enough, so is the National Socialist German

Workers Party. But what could this NSR have been? It is not to be found in the *Encyclopedia of the Third Reich*, it is ignored by Toland and Shirer and Irving and Speer and Fest and everyone else I've read. An Austrian acquaintance, himself a former Nazi, comes to my rescue. "That was an illegal group," he writes. "Underground. Mostly kids to begin with, it started in the army."

A week after his letter I come across a scholarly and comparatively obscure book, and there it is, the elusive NSR, finally documented in print. The group is noted as being instrumental, particularly in Graz, as working toward—agitating for?—the *Anschluss*. Since the historian who wrote the book merely names the association without elucidating further, I write to his London publisher. Was that possibly some sort of veterans' organization, I ask—hoping my Austrian source is mistaken—a group of soldiers and former soldiers meeting once a year at a picnic, boozing it up and reminiscing about army days? "Quite definitely not a veterans' organization," is the historian's reply. "The National Socialist Soldiers' Ring was comprised of National Socialist cells of activists in the army and the police." A secret underground group, whose members saw themselves as revolutionaries. "He clearly joined in the army," adds my Austrian acquaintance in a follow-up letter. "And then he stayed in it, once he switched to the police. He must have continued to actively work for the NSR, that's how they finally somehow got it on his record."

And there is the second photograph from my father's army years. He
is amid the military band of what I presume to be the Ninth Alpine
Hunters Regiment. It is a klutzy-looking group, assembled under a
large tree, in front of one of the miniature chapels common in
rural Austria. (They flank country roads or stand, forlorn, in the
middle of a forest, high up on a mountain—chapels the size of a
phone booth housing a crucifix or a plaster Virgin, and wild
flowers in a chipped vase.) The farmers—onlookers in the
background—wear suits, it's Sunday.

The tree shelters the entire band. Someone has clearly given thought to logistics, this is no snapshot. Twenty men in rumpled uniforms stand in a row, waiting uncomfortably and patiently as if for a train, hands folded stiffly over their genitals or behind their backs; four more kneel awkwardly, two drummers recline in the foreground, an elbow each propped on their instruments.

I have shown the photograph to friends, asking each time, "Which one seems most sure of himself, posing instead of just standing willy-nilly, striking an attitude for the camera?" They always pick him.

He wears a mustache now. Is he twenty-one? Twenty-two? He is the only one of the group whose arms are crossed in front of his chest, his weight rests on one leg while the other one is thrust forward and bent slightly at the knee. The flared bell of a French horn is cradled casually in the crook of one arm. He looks straight into the camera. There is nothing dreamy about him now, but something dashing instead and something amused, he will burst out laughing as soon as the shutter has clicked. This young man is at ease, assured. If he is neither, he has become adept at putting on a very good front.

Since untold millions on more than one continent have been slaughtered in the name of Communism, and since the abominations that continue to be committed by Communist governments have nothing to do with the tenets formulated by the original theorists of this ideology, I assume that any contemporary Communist must be aware of upholding a set of ideals that has yet to be put into practice. Even so, I count among my acquaintances several people to whom the label "revolutionary Marxist" or "Communist revolutionary" carries overtones of romantic appeal. And while a book called *The Romance of American Communism*

does not cause a stir in Manhattan in 1979, I find it difficult to envision the windows of my local bookstore decked out with volumes entitled *The Appeal of Fascism* or, specifically, *The Romance of National Socialism.*

It would horrify me to encounter such a sight. And if an otherwise intelligent acquaintance of mine professes a kinship to Communism, that's fine with me. I do not ask if he would like to *live* in the Soviet Republic of New York, I listen politely, and sometimes with interest, to the old litanies. The mulling over of such abstractions is harmless as far as it goes, its end product most often the writing of articles for small journals—as honorable a way of spending one's time as any.

But the objective distance with which we generally study the theories and early phases of political movements does not hold when the movement under scrutiny is National Socialism. The fire ignited, stoked, fanned, and finally unleashed under the aegis of this movement left so vast and desolate a landscape of human suffering that an objective consideration of its other aspects is nearly impossible. "They made the trains run on time" is the single most sickening sentence in the world.

To me, both Communism and National Socialism are drearily devoid of all romantic appeal. But while I have yet to lose sleep over the appeal of Communism, I am engaged in the slippery pursuit of attempting to fathom why my father joined the Nazis. A woman not her father's daughter, a woman unlike me, might have put aside being cut off at the age of seventeen, might have tried his patience and her luck again, might have asked, carefully choosing her words, at twenty-three, or at twenty-eight, or at thirty-two. I could not, and I regret it. What I am left with is conjecture.

Only when I turn the question upside down do I feel on firmer ground. What might have *prevented* him from becoming a Nazi? Or: For what reasons might he *not* have joined? Or: What might have *repelled* him? These answers seem simpler. Nothing. None. Nothing.

A great many Austrians of my father's youth were driven by what is commonly expressed in an abstract noun. At the best of times, it is not a one-definition word. At that time, in that place, is carried extraordinary emotional weight. Nationalism.

Prospering citizens of a nation at peace and threatened by no one can afford to take their country for granted, to be casually critical of this or that national quirk or policy, to appreciate virtues and values of other countries, perhaps all countries. Hungry and deprived citizens of an impoverished and beleaguered country tend to assume a different stance. The perception of oneself as surrounded by enemies generally belongs in the realm of psychopathology, under the heading of paranoia, and a severely ill paranoiac can be dangerous to those around him. But if this perception is fostered by prolonged, intense, and physical deprivation, pathology gives way to dreadful "health." Faced with the *reality* of being stuck in a dead-end hallway encircled by hostile forces, even normally thoughtful people tend to abandon the rational point of view, which would hold that the nations causing the suffering must surely consist of humans just as nice and ordinary as one's underweight neighbors up and down the street.

To have lost a war is difficult. To be excluded from the family of nations in peacetime, and for years, is lethal. If a war has long been over, and one's powerful "former" enemies continue to behave in a relentlessly vindictive manner, it is tempting to conclude: During the war, those enemies aimed to defeat my country; now they aim to destroy it, and me. Driven to such a conclusion, one fears and hates one's enemies, and one tends to fall back on a vastly stepped up, near-mythical loyalty to what is left: one's own backyard, one's country.

But Nationalism was not enough. Before you can spare the time and energy to be proud of your family, you need to see all of its members eat a full meal in front of your eyes. Before you can be proud of your country, you need to see that you and your neighbors and friends are able to find a job and a place to live. It also helps to know that you can afford a doctor if your children get sick, and, should you as a line worker get mangled for life, that those children will not have to take turns selling pencils on the street.

A desperate desire to be protected, to help and protect one another—who else was going to do it?—that desire had an abstract noun label as well. It was called Socialism.

"We were as ready to believe in Socialism as the Reds themselves," says one of my aging former Nazi relatives. "There was only one thing I couldn't swallow, and nobody I knew could either, and that was the international thing. International anything had never done me any good. The 'international brotherhood of workers,' and 'workers of the world unite,' well, that sure didn't include *us*, they made that clear enough. Our Russian 'brothers' and our French 'brothers,' great revolutionaries all, they agreed to the embargo and to Versailles just as gladly as the capitalist Americans, all of them were happy to watch us starve. Not one of those countries out there wanted a thing to do with us. Some 'brotherhood.' But when people started talking about throwing 'international' out, and keeping the rest of what Socialism stood for, using it how *we* needed it, well . . ."

Nationalism and Socialism, Socialism and Nationalism, Nationalism and Socialism, until the two abstractions merged. This notion was far from new, but it had only been yet another dusty notion kicked around in dusty pamphlets. When it caught on, the solution to a previously insoluble dilemma seemed suddenly obvious. What had been contradictory ideological absolutes—Nationalism by definition excluding Socialism, which by definition excluded Nationalism—became one ideal. It took hold of people's imagination as a revolutionary idea, the magic combination, a daring dream. First entranced were the young.

Whenever we see photographs of Nazis in history books or on television documentaries, there is always Himmler, the nightmare schoolteacher, grossly fat Göring drooling through obscene sneers,

Goebbels, a hybrid of rodent and buzzard, Hitler himself. Has he ever, in a single photograph, looked anything but ludicrous? Either he rants, a lunatic; or he fits into his entourage—well-fed, self-satisfied, beaming, middle-aged men at the top of their power.

But when my father became a Nazi he was half the age I am now, closer in age to my sixteen-year-old daughter than to me, half the age of most of my friends. He was nowhere near middle-aged, he was far from fat.

The largest meeting of early-bird Austrian National Socialists took place in the summer of 1923, in Salzburg. Enthusiasts had traveled cross-country to write up a slate, they wanted to run one of their own for office. The convention was important enough for Hitler to make an appearance in his former fatherland. The same man who would, ten years later, win a plurality of Germany's electorate through the familiar barnstorming process of holding babies for photographers and giving six speeches a day in six different towns, now checked out this crowd and, no fool, swiftly decided that Austrian Nazis were to abstain from the elections, "according to the party's program, which rejects all parliamentarianism." A Colonel Bauer expressed a better reason for abstention. "A lot of people were there," was how he put it, "but most of them were between seventeen and nineteen." And not even ardent adolescents were allowed either to run for office or to vote.

Long before their middle-aged parents edged into the party, cautiously, sideways, young people were professing themselves National Socialists in masses. When the Nazis finally took over, they pronounced themselves, and justifiably so, the "Party of Youth."

My father's generation had, in childhood, lived through the deprivations of the war and postwar years, and had, in adolescence, observed how dismally unable to function the adults' "democracy" was. They had watched their elders be consumed by the effort of keeping families alive, politically ineffectual, cringing with fear.

What young Nazis had in common above all was a fervent desire *to do.* The first thing to be done was to throw out whatever one's parents' had tried. Good riddance to the monarchy, which so many of the old ones still mourned and which my father's generation barely remembered, and let's throw out this mess that passes for a government now, this pathetic democracy imposed on Austria by its enemies, surely with the intention of keeping Austria crippled forever. Namby-pamby, dilly-dallying old men, going over the same issue month after month, no one able to achieve a majority, no one ever getting a thing done. Democracy was a joke. Something else would have to take its place, this was not the way to live out one's life, what was needed was a drastic change.

In terms of idealism, my father's generation of early Nazis holds its own as compared to the most devoted of Whole Earth purists of our 1960s. Unfortunately, an idealistic dunce is a dunce nonetheless, an idealistic pickpocket a thief, an idealistic bore as dull as the bore who happens to be an opportunist; idealism per se leads nowhere.

This is what they wanted. A body of government to consult on all issues, yes, by all means, but *one* person empowered to make decisions. If a decision had to be made about an increase of ten Schillings a month for the pension of a soldier's widow, do it. No more parliamentary sessions stretching over months and years, debating the comparative virtues of nine Schillings over eleven, each party far more interested in keeping another party from winning a point than in settling the issue, while the woman starved. Many decisions were begging to be made.

There would be one people, one leader. The people of this ideal country would love one another, each inhabitant would, after all, be a member of one family, loyal to the rest of the clan. (I do not know if my father, when thinking his idealistic Nazi thoughts, ever gave a glance in the direction of his brother Eduard, but I doubt it. Idealists tend to be weak in the area of common sense.)

The shining new symbol of this idealistic new order of the future, its guiding principle and First Commandment would be,

"The Common Good before the Private Good." Everyone would share, all classes would work together. ("When Hitler first carried on about how we were all going to be equal, 'the workers of the head and the workers of the fist,' well, I just wrote that off as talk," a retired factory worker from Frankfurt told me in 1977. "Class is class, and class is everything to Germans. But I was wrong. There was a camaraderie, the kind we had in the trenches, except that after the war's over you forget about it again. That handful of years under Hitler was the one time in my life when I got the same respect as a teacher.") What's more, everyone would lead a wholesome life, enthusiasts would jog before breakfast, women were beautiful without artifice, makeup was French, anyway. All would believe in nutritious food, a fit body, the healthy outdoors, each other, and the man who would lead them.

He would lead them along a path of sacrifice at first, but toward great glory. They would put their hopes in tomorrow—might as well, there was nothing to hope for today. They would hope and work for tomorrow, all they'd need was confidence, if only they stuck together they could drag this unholy mess that the old ones had made of their country out of the morass, and clean it and buff it and polish it to a shine, a brand-new gem, let the past be damned.

And yes, National Socialists were anti-Semitic. In fact, anti-Semitism may have been the one common denominator among all Austrian parties, from the extreme and moderate left, over middle-of-the-road conservatives, to the various factions of the extreme right. Anti-Semitism pervaded Austria's political parties because anti-Semitism pervaded Austria. While a hostile and clearly defined tradition of religious anti-Semitism had, during much of the nineteenth century, subsided into a vague sentiment, increasingly now, this traditional kind of anti-Semitism was giving way to a different kind, the worst kind, an anti-Semitism based more and more on fear.

A farmer who barely produces enough for his family to survive does not take it lightly when a group of Polish Jews digs unripe potatoes from his field. That the refugees had been driven into Austria by extraordinary savagery in their own country, and that they were near starvation and desperate, might have struck even an impoverished farmer as reasons enough to sell them food. But in 1919, or 1920, the loss of half a potato crop in July meant that the farmer's family starved in January. And if there were Austrian Christians among the marauders in his field, that farmer would remember their thievery far less vividly than the same act committed by equally hungry Jewish foreigners who looked clearly, even strikingly, "different."

It might not have occurred to such a farmer to complain (as members of the urban middle class were fond of doing) that most newspapers were owned by Jews, or that Jews dominated Austria's cultural and intellectual life. However, he would have known who owned the railroads. And whether or not this farmer truly longed to visit his sister, who had happened to move to a different province, he would have blamed the Rothschilds for his inability to afford the fare.

His city counterpart, a carpenter or a shoemaker, lived next door to the members of the proletariat. At night, he watched his neighbors come home, exhausted from a day working on someone else's machines for someone else's gain. During the day he watched his goods be passed up in favor of newly mass-produced items, he let his journeyman go, he faced the fact that he would not be able to afford the raw materials for his trade for longer than another six weeks. He was deeply aware of the ever-narrowing gap between himself and the wretches next door, and he would not have perceived industrialization in terms of economic development. He would blame Jewish industrialists instead.

His counterpart among those Austrian workers, who had

managed to forge unions, may have felt a measure of security, trusting in the protection of contracts. He may even have looked forward to flexing some muscle under the spell of a newly gained class consciousness. But day after day, month after month, year after year, a seemingly inexhaustible stream of fresh labor continued to pour into Austrian cities from the east. Polish refugees were willing to work for a fraction of the hourly wage, agreed on after sometimes violent struggles between workers and management. The Austrian factory worker would watch a recently forged solidarity crumble, and he would lose his job.

A good part of Austria's middle class, nearly all of Austria's lower-middle class, and a good part of Austria's working class perceived—*perceived*—itself to be under severe pressure, equally threatened from above and below; *perceived*, furthermore: above and below were Jews.

Given what shaped him, and his time and place, I can understand why my father might have joined the Nazis. I do not understand why he remained one for over two decades. I do not want to try. I am too frightened by the specter of such rigidity, I listen to its echo in myself: an allegiance pledged, one's lot cast, no dissenting thought or feeling allowed to enter one's mind or heart, worship at the altar of the most repressive of gods, loyalty as an absolute.

There are all those sociologists' studies of prejudice, cleverly worded tests devised and administered, answers broken down into categories, analyzed, evaluated. And scholars have vividly described those periods of history in which prejudice flourished, and given us various reasons of why here but not there, why then and not earlier, all those reasons of economics and personality structure and religion and patriotism and how threatened (not necessarily by Jews; just threatened at large) Gentiles feel at any one point. And there are nightmare libraries full of books on the results of prejudice in my lifetime alone.

We've got them down pat, the whys and the wheres, the causes, conditions, and effects. But where is the body of research and knowledge, telling us what to do about it?

If I had a phobia—of heights, dogs, you name it—there would not only be an established psychiatric manner of dealing with my complaint, there would also be all sorts of newly discovered methods of treatment to choose from; research in phobias is booming. Unraveling at the sound of Yiddish seems as irrational to me, as deserving of the label "phobia," as an inability to look down from the Empire State Building. But how is it being treated? When will scholars and psychiatrists and sociologists stop measuring and studying and reflecting on what percentage of blue-collar workers (and white-collar workers, and veterans, and college students) believe that "money is their god," and start working on a method of treatment? It is as if we're going around and around, describing the onset of palpitations at the height of five feet, or the first appearance of the rash typical of a disease called measles. *Describing* measles: who is most prone to it, how long do outbreaks last, number of casualties, theories of what brought about the very last epidemic, and oft-repeated rhetoric about how measles are a curse of humanity.

A merely descriptive approach would not be tolerated for either phobias or measles. We have vaccines for the latter, a whole range of psychiatric services for the former. People gather in groups to become more assertive, less angry, more affectionate; to end smoking, drinking, overeating, impotence, drug addiction, and who knows what else. There are no consciousness-raising groups for bigots.

Of course, prejudice is not considered to be in the same category as either measles or phobias. At worst, it is simply a taboo, to be exorcised by being ignored. At best it is a sin, my very own responsibility to be struggled with at the peril of my immortal soul; entitling me to absolution whenever I repent and confess, and an admonition to try harder next time.

Never to hold on to money, to laugh at the idea of savings accounts, immediately to spend what you manage to earn, and to spend every cent not essential for staying alive on the one thing on earth that lasts: dirt; land; a chunk of Earth itself—my father had been taught these lessons twice. He did not draw his Seiler Bunker conclusions until years later, and then moved by powers only marginally connected to money, but he did draw them.

The first inflation, culminating in 1923, was dreadful, ghastly, mind-numbing—but also unique, a disaster no one imagined could ever repeat itself. When it was over, Austrians began to save again. They opened new accounts, they stuck to a regimen of putting aside an inviolable sum each week, small as it may be. Then came the second inflation.

Neither the first nor the second, less than a decade later, was the sort of inflation that currently causes concern among Americans. "Seven percent one quarter, then nine, double digits now, where the hell will it end. . . ."

Just like the first inflation my father lived through, the second one, too, did not bother with a stately progression of seven percent here, nine there; it was a more radical process. Not that it erupted overnight. Still, all it took was a couple of years. No one could help see it coming, no one was able to head it off. When it hit, it was a catastrophe.

Let us assume, by way of illustration, that I am a married man, and that my wife and I have three children under the age of ten. I'm a line supervisor for a battery company in Brooklyn, my wife works three afternoons a week in a neighborhood beauty shop. For the past five years we've been living in a semidetached house in Queens, almost a third of it paid up, thanks in part to my parents-in-law, they've been a great help.

My wife and I have $8,000 in our savings account. Mostly we don't go to movies, we watch television, play with the kids. I gave up bowling, all I drink is a couple of beers. Sometimes we kid around about taking off, just clean out the account and go on a trip, something. But we were both brought up thrifty and you don't mind scrimping a little if you know why you're doing it. You watch the food bills, vacations we spend at my brother's in Florida, it all adds up.

Except that today I stop at the subway booth to buy my token and it costs $6,000. There is a deli next to the plant, a coffee-to-go, light, no sugar, is $4,500. My wife bought a loaf of bread, the supermarket brand, you want to know what it cost? It cost eight thousand, one hundred, and fifty dollars. What we saved up in eleven years, starting the day we got back from our honeymoon, it's not enough to buy a loaf of bread.

While this example gives an idea of the general proportions at work, it fails to mention the farcical amounts of money in circulation, and it is hopelessly inadequate in conveying what these inflations were like, near and at their peak.

The battery-company man from Queens will soon stop worrying about the price of bread. His weekly salary will be in ten figures, but he will barely manage to buy potatoes for his family. On payday, he will run from his plant to the subway, push his way through a panic-stricken crowd, charge down the stairs four steps at a time. If the doors of the train have closed in his face, he might pound them with his fists, deprived of the option open to his European counterparts, groups of whom would cling to the outsides of streetcars. He will know what a ten-minute wait for the next train means. The weekly salary check in his hand has just lost three quarters of the buying power it would have represented had he been able to get to the bank, and a nearby food store, on the train now moving out of the station without him.

Americans find it difficult to imagine such a turn of events, since this sort of inflation has not yet occurred in their country. What I find most elusive is trying to speculate on how long, and how vividly, the financial equivalent of an earthquake hitting the top of the Richter scale remains a force among the private memories of each of those human beings who combine to make up that organism we call a nation.

While the inflations affected everyone, they hit the middle, lower-middle, and working class hardest, and, of course, anyone living on a pension. But if the financial blow had been catastrophic, there occurred yet another loss, no less devastating or real but largely invisible, not to be charted on graphs, outside the realm—at least for the moment—of statisticians' wizardry. To some degree as an outcome of the first inflation, but certainly after the second one, a sliding began. There had been certain assumptions, held on to through war and deprivation, the kind so taken for granted that they were only alluded to, one was aware of saying nothing new. "Things have a way of turning out for the best." "God helps those who help themselves." "Everything looks better after a good night's sleep." Humble and timeworn code words, meant to express what one did not voice in the course of ordinary conversation: the hope for a small amount of predictability inherent in one's life, a modest confidence in one's ability to survive.

But as the nation's monetary currency plummeted through its month-by-month and finally minute-by-minute devaluation, attitudes often considered unrelated to money began a slithering of their own, began to mirror, in their rate of decline, that of one's ever more worthless paper currency. One's sense of self-esteem does not, for the most part, crumble overnight. The earthquakes meant devastation, not the end. But there was unchartable damage.

"If I work as hard as I possibly can, I will be able to support myself and my family." This belief had, despite evidence to the contrary, still been a given for an Austrian waiter or factory worker, teacher or salesclerk. The second inflation, coupled with massive unemployment, finally made the folly of such an assumption clear.

There are few more powerful invitations to nihilism than the conviction: it makes no difference what I do; what I need is beyond my reach, what I want is beside the point, what I stand for means nothing to me or to anyone else, it does not matter what I do.

A great many Austrians and Germans needed and wanted nothing more urgently than to be told, *Damn it, we matter and it matters what we do! We are going to stick together, we will take care of our own, there is nothing—do you hear me?—there is nothing we can't do! By God, think of our grand history, think of our past glory, think of this great country of ours, let the world watch us astound the world!*

Overnight, a new genre of jokes was born. To repeat these jokes to everyone you met, and to hear half a dozen new ones daily, was a balm. In line before soup kitchens people reminded each other, "The situation is desperate, but not serious."

My favorite inflation joke is the one about the man who buys a loaf of bread for a million, trades it for a Mercedes, sells that for two million, buys a machine gun to hold up a bank and finds, when he gets there, that the bank has been turned into a bakery, selling a loaf of bread for three million, but only to customers who bring their own flour.

My second favorite is not a joke. An Austrian friend of mine says it is a true story that he heard from the friend of a friend of the woman.

This woman is on her way to the store; she carries a wicker basket. Eventually she will cart home her groceries in this basket, but now it is filled with money; the number of banknotes she needs to buy the ingredients for her family's dinner would not fit into a wallet or purse.

Halfway between her house and the grocer's she meets a neighbor. The women stop and greet each other warmly, and the woman carrying the basket proceeds to tell her friend a spicy tidbit involving the female boarder on the ground floor of her building, and the building's generally disliked, and married, landlord. The denouement of the story proves to be awkward to relate without the use of indiscreet language; what's more, this storyteller prefers to describe certain matters with the help of her eloquent arms gliding through the air at just the right angle and speed. She sets down the basket and finishes her story with all the mimicry at her command. Her neighbor is shocked and delighted, she laughs so hard that her breasts shake, noticeably, in public. Each woman offers greetings to be conveyed to the other's husband, then the neighbor walks away. The storyteller bends down to pick up her basket, but all that is left, dumped in a heap on the sidewalk, is the money. A thief has stolen her basket.

I have heard this story three or four times. According to whim, so I had assumed, my Austrian source either ends the tale as I just did, or adds a concluding chapter.

In the appended version the grieving woman happens to be wearing an apron and fashions a sack of it, gathering up the apron's hem. She grabs up the money, fistful after fistful, and stuffs it into her makeshift bag. Since grocers expect customers to provide their own containers, she carries her groceries as she has earlier carried her money. She puts the two eggs she has bought on top of the little pile, which she hugs, inside the apron, against her stomach.

On her way home she morosely berates herself. Setting the fool thing down in the first place, on the sidewalk yet, what a careless thing to do, her husband will let her hear about it for weeks and she will deserve it, gossiping when she had better things to do. . . . But her thoughts are interrupted by a curious sensation. She pulls in her stomach and, as unobtrusively as possible, moves her upper body first to the left, then to the right. No doubt about it, her newly bought square of lard has melted through her apron and dress, her underclothes stick to her skin, she is soaked with melting lard.

She stops in mid-step and stands stiffly in the middle of the sidewalk. All at once, her remorse and shame have left her, her cheeks flush a deep red, she is beside herself, furious.

As suddenly and as unaccountably she laughs out loud, the heartiest, most brazen belly laugh imaginable. Two feet to her left is the entrance to a bar. She has never been inside alone, but her husband used to take her there, they had not been married yet, he had courted her shyly.

An agreeable bartender takes a small fish, which had been destined to become her family's dinner, in exchange for a generous glass of slivovitz. She drinks the first half in a single gulp, the second half slowly, sip after tiny insect sip.

At the end of the evening she combs her hair and powders herself; there had been times when she had been able to make things up to her husband. But when she gets into bed, he is asleep. She gives herself over to how the slivovitz has etched its way down her throat, enjoying little sips, no longer caring what people thought: What *is* the woman carrying in her apron, a farm tramp in the city, and isn't her skirt stained in front? She remembers the moment when she stopped minding the warm lard sliding down her thighs, pleasant really, how could a day that was interrupted by such a mishap round out so pleasantly?

From then on she uses her son's knapsack to carry money to the store and eventually, of course, the inflation ends.

I tell my Austrian friend that I prefer the appended version and he says, "I never tell that one to Americans."

"No?"

"They're too sentimental," he says, "always carrying on about the 'human element' in a story, that's how they put it when I was over there last. A perplexing phrase. Is it still being bandied about?"

"*Sentimental!*" I say. "And coming from *you!*"

"Look," he says, "of course we're sentimental too. But we're sentimental in such a different way."

"I don't have the faintest idea of what you're talking about," I say, as the image of the Empire State Building rises before me, atrociously lit, gloriously beautiful. I suppress my vision.

"You've been over there a long time," he says, "but you haven't shaken it yet."

"What a pity," I say. "Tell me, what haven't I managed to shake?"

"And you won't, either," he says. "It's in you. It doesn't matter where your body lives out its life. A wicker basket you can set down, and it may or may not disappear, but you haven't been to a church in years, right?"

"Right," I say, mystified now.

"But Catholicism lives on inside you, nonetheless."

"What a pleasant theory," I say and laugh. "Faith-as-gallstone-at-rest. Where did I ever get the idea that the belief business was such a time-consuming affair, shifts around the clock and all that?"

He smiles indulgently.

"You've been an American citizen for how long now?"

"Ten years, twelve."

"The former Ingeborg Seiler of Graz, Austria, has been a certified citizen—"

"*Naturalized*," I say, surprised by the petty edge to my voice. "A naturalized citizen of the United States."

"I am glad this pleases you," he says, and his voice is warm and devoid of sarcasm. "Listen to me," he says, and puts his hand on mine. "I worry about it. There is this streak of yours, how you throw your arm around a choice you've made and hug it to you, which has served you well. But at times you don't just hold on, you close your eyes, too."

"Oh, dear," I say and reach for my glass. "And just when I thought I was beginning to mend my ways. But if that's all you're worried about, there's reason to celebrate as well, isn't there? Think of how far I've come, and so grievously handicapped, too."

"I am afraid for you," he says. "You will keep right on making yourself unhappy until you come to a peace about the . . . fact, that you will always be, first and foremost, an Austrian."

"But you are so *wrong*," I say. "I am *not*, not anymore, I haven't been an Austrian for—"

"Please," he says, "please. It isn't up to you, don't you see? Over there, all you own is a piece of paper which proves, to you and anyone else who cares, that you are entitled to vote and requested to pay taxes in a country you picked. But Austria picked you first. To fight this fact, or to treasure it, or to ignore it, well, that's up to you. Austria doesn't care, and the Church doesn't either."

What does he want from me? I think, tired now and cross, the kind of mood that prompted Mark, at the age of three or four, to kick at table legs in passing, I'd give up both countries to have him back and every last church in the world; you've had too much wine, I tell myself, and yesterday that wretched flight, how will I get a cab at this hour?

Out loud I say, "You still haven't told me why Americans don't deserve to hear the second version of your basket story."

He says nothing. I look at my hands, at his, the taxi question nags; will I wander around town, trying to find one of their quaint little pastures, five pompous, black Mercedes' hanging out in a chummy row and not one cruising the streets, what an inane system, typical, why on earth do I keep coming back? see my lazy brother? in twenty years he's managed to write me four times, and

does *he* ever come and see *me?* take a streetcar then, you do like
those, how small schoolgirls wave their passes at the conductor,
never a pause in their giggly talk like little splashes of water; but it's
different late at night, rumbling through dead streets, halting at a
deserted stop, doors opening, doors open, doors open, doors still
open, what can this fool of a driver be waiting for? the ritual
repeated at every godforsaken stop, though I am the lone passenger
and ensconced as if for the night, and though the driver sees each
desolate stop well in advance; we cater to an invisible rush-hour
crowd, standing room only, halfhearted jostling, a brightly lit car
full of weary and patient ghosts; those two at the door are familiar
to me, and the one to my right as well, faces solid as flesh and
dearer to me than my own, Jesus, a Checker, let me flag down a
Checker, let me scrunch down in the dark and be safe from all
ghosts for as long as I keep my eyes on the dirty sign, *keep feet off
jump seats. . . .*

". . . finally turned eighty last month," he is saying in a low
voice. "And for me, the essence of being Austrian is graceful
resignation. The basket woman knew that. She scrambled her two
eggs that night, and stretched them with water and powdered milk,
and poured the sauce on pieces of bread."

"You know this story very well," I say slowly. "Obnoxiously
well, to be precise. Far too well. If I were you, I'd put all this
nonsense in a nice, juicy novel, lard-on-thighs, that sort of thing."

"I had an affair with her," he says. "Not an affair, a love. Years
after the basket thing. Her husband left her, but then he came
back."

I didn't mean a word I said, my dear friend, forgive me, I
thought. But I did not say it out loud, and now he is dead too.

"My father would have scoffed at the word 'graceful,' " I said
instead. "And he would have hated the word 'resignation.' "

"He may well have," said my friend. "As you know, I never met
him. But we can only go through so many earthquakes. There
comes a point when there is finally too much rubble around to

bother with. You stop trying to erect ethereal constructions, you build a shelter instead. He went on, did he not? He concentrated on what was left, and he lived by that. Once we've been made to realize that illusions are a comfort like any other, it behooves us to take their loss in stride, and without pretending that the loss is temporary."

"You've got him all wrong," I said.

"Very well," he said. "After all, I never knew him. But the basket woman I knew well, and not in a hundred years would it have occurred to this woman to point out the 'human element' in any story. Tell me, *what else is there?*"

"Oh, all right then," I said. "So you've made up your mind about Americans. I suppose they'll somehow manage to live with that."

"I know only a few and none of them well," he said. "And the half dozen or so to whom I've told it seemed to enjoy the story. Money dumped on a sidewalk, they like that, they laugh. But when the chuckles die down the questions start, always the same questions. Instead of taking the trouble to leave the money behind, wouldn't it have made more sense just to pick up the basket and run? Did not the thief increase his risk, fiddling at the woman's feet, needlessly drawing attention to himself? And if the money could buy any groceries at all, even a few, why would the thief . . . You see, that is their practical side; it saves them from drowning in sentimentality. But there isn't an Austrian alive who would ask a single one of those questions. And if somebody doesn't understand the *thief* of the story, what is the point of talking about the woman?"

Americans tend to lump Austrians and Germans into a single group. One period among many that make this practice seem inappropriate is that of the 1930s. In Germany, Hitler took power in 1933; the five years that passed before he annexed Austria were very different for Germans than for their neighbors to the south.

"A year after Hitler took over, out there, as we used to say, Austrian workers went to the barricades," recalls a man who knew my father. "The Reds gave it a valiant try. Between the inflation, and unemployment having hit bottom, it just came to a boiling point. So they sent the workers out in the streets, Go and yell your heads off, protest! It was easy sending them in the streets, they had nothing else to do anyway. Getting them to go home again was harder. We had a cozy little civil war on our hands.

"Our inspiring Socialist leaders, Adler, Deutsch, you name them, all of them Jews, they got a hold of the party's cash box and hopped on a train for France. The minor officials, Christians, they were hanged or shot. And the rank-and-file Red, the unemployed laborer who had dreamed of a Socialist revolution and a Socialist state, he sat in jail and fingered his bloody bandages. 'What do you think our Socialist leaders are doing right now?' was the first line of a joke going around. 'They are hard at work, sitting in Paris cafés, writing new revolutionary tracts.'

"Some Austrian Nazis gave it a try, too, but their silly little *Putsch* was over even faster; and along it came, our glorious Austro-Fascism. I was fourteen, fifteen. These days, thank God, boys that age talk about girls and soccer, not that we didn't. But we talked about other things too, under our breath, of course, and always in the far corner of the schoolyard.

"The Clericals, the Conservatives, they'd taken over, the government was 'Black.' 'Christian Socials' they called themselves. Our report cards had a new category, 'Attendance at Mass.' You missed Mass once, you stayed after school. You missed it a second time, you tried to find a different school. I'd been put in an orphanage run by the Lutherans, and before my father died he'd been with the railroads, they were notorious Reds, so teachers kept bringing up my father's job or asked if I'd turned Lutheran yet, and being a Lutheran, well, that was only half a step away from being a heretic, only *our* Church was Christian.

"The worst of them was the priest who taught Religion, that subject was more important for your academic standing than Chemistry or German. He called me up front once for an exam, that was six months before the *Anschluss*. He asks me a question, something about Kant and Nietzsche, he liked tearing those two apart, heretics they were and idiots. But before I can open my mouth he says, 'How dare you stand like that in my presence, you have the posture of a streetcar conductor, go back to your seat.' Because I hadn't clicked my heels. I got an F in Religion on my report card, that was a death sentence for a *Gymnasium* student at the time. Half a year later, when the German troops 'liberated' us, well, they really did liberate me. And to get any sort of work, you had to show up with your confession paper. . . ."

Reds and Blacks and Adler and Deutsch I had read about in numerous books and theses. These sources had, as a rule, presented the historical events embroiling these parties and leaders from a perspective radically unlike the one with which I am confronted now, on an azure-sky Austrian summer afternoon, only months away from the 1980s. There was no point in interrupting this particular man to ask, "If *you* had been the leader of a revolution that failed, would *you* have stuck around, waiting for the regime's executioners? And since the party had fallen apart, would *you* have left its cash box behind, for your enemies to gloat over?" Now I interrupt him after all: confession papers, described from whatever perspective, are new to me.

"Oh, you know, a scrap of paper signed by the priest after you'd made your confession. If you missed one Saturday night's absolution, you were no upstanding member of the Christian Social Party, you didn't deserve a job. And there were very few around. Some family men with children to feed would have killed for a job, given half a chance.

"My older brother earned his title of *Diplomingenieur* in '36, the year our mother died, he had to put off the final exams because of the funeral. There was no job for him, no unemployment, no welfare. At God-knows-what sacrifice our mother had put him through five years at the university after eight years at the *Gymnasium* and nobody so much as let him split wood in a backyard.

"Times like these, you find out how resourceful you are. Anybody who fancied himself musically inclined became a street singer. Housewives would open a window facing the tenement courtyard, listen to a song, applaud a little, maybe throw a *Groschen* at the singer five floors down. Street-singing was illegal, but neighborhoods looked out for those paupers, anybody who still had a job thought, Tomorrow *I* could be down there, scratching pennies. So people'd yell, 'Cop's halfway up the block, you've got a minute and a half.'

"Your father was the most closed-mouthed man I've ever met, but he told me a detail from that period. Maybe it came up when I mentioned to him that my brother had tried it as a street singer, he didn't make it though, he never could carry a tune. Your father's precinct, like every other precinct, was overrun by street singers. One day a cop—your father didn't mention names—got mad. He called together as many guys as were around and said, 'The hell with this garbage. I'm not hauling in one more skin-and-bone hooker who's just sold her ass for a cup of coffee, and when I hear another nightingale caterwauling in some alley, I swear I'll stick my fists in my ears.'

"Word got around, the precinct got a small fund together. Each hooker and street singer too obvious to be ignored by the cop on the beat, every out-of-work carpenter, stenographer, and *Diplominge-nieur*, got taken to the station and fed a bowl of goulash and a roll. When they were done eating the sergeant would say, 'On your mother's life, don't let me catch sight of you in this precinct again.' That's what times were like, flat out, flat out on the floor.

"And every year we heard new and more amazing stories about what the Germans were up to. All through the twenties they'd been in the same mess we'd been in, except now we were worse off than ever, while all of a sudden they were working, they were eating, they were taking *vacations*, we couldn't even believe it. Factory workers and their wives and kids cruising down some river, who'd ever heard of anything like that before?"

Between 1934 and 1938, the structure of Austria's First Republic was simple. No elections, government by decree, a one-party state—and all without help from Adolf Hitler. I have thanked God and luck that the world at large was not interested in Austria's form of government during those years, and I am grateful that Austria's spokesmen after the Second World War managed to convey to our occupiers a fantasy version of Austria's pre-Hitler government: unfortunate little Austria, Europe's first democracy to be slugged to the ground by the treacherous Nazi Huns from the north. Had this ruse not been accepted, how would its occupiers have dealt with the country of my birth?

Gratefulness acknowledged, I believe that truth was not an issue. There seems little merit to an interpretation of the *Anschluss* in terms of a brute-force occupation. What appears more accurate is an interpretation in terms of an agreeable union on one level and, on another, the exchange of a corrupt, wretchedly inept, and totalitarian government for a government that was totalitarian, corrupt, and eminently successful.

The sham of a helpless democracy threatened by *Panzer* tanks about to flatten the Alps served Austria and its postwar occupiers equally well. Austrians were able to tell themselves and the world, "The Germans invaded us." Occupiers, East and West alike, were happy enough to accept minor alterations of history in view of Austria's strategic position in a very important and brand-new War, the Cold one.

It was under its Christian Social government that Austrians first became acquainted with concentration camps, whose prisoners spanned the political spectrum considered disruptive by Austria's First Republic. Rabble-rousing (or potentially rabble-rousing) Communists, National Socialists, and Socialists, who had not managed to avoid the attention of the state, were referred to, in guards' parlance—adjectives chosen according to a strictly democratic notion of vocabulary—as those goddamn Commies, those goddamn Nazis, those goddamn Reds.

The building I live in has a basement laundry room, its walls cluttered with advertisements for dinette sets, "cheap, moving this month," and similar notices. This one caught my attention: "12-year-old-boy wants to run errands; reliable; good dog-walker; 50¢ a trip."

That's how I met Andy, who is preparing for his Bar Mitzvah, memorizing Hebrew and worrying about a speech he is expected to prepare. He has become dear to me over these months of seeing hardly anyone else, and he knows I am writing, "something to do with the Second World War." One day he asks me, "Are you an

Aryan?" I laugh and say, "Oh, Lord! Where on earth did you pick up *that* word?" He says, "Well, I don't really know much about that war, but I've heard that the Christians sort of got away, and the Jews got killed, and the Aryans were the ones who killed them."

I say, trying to feel my way, slowly, "Actually, the Christians and the Aryans were mostly the same people." And he says, "Are you an Aryan, then?" And I say, "Well, it's such a silly way of categorizing people . . . yes. By birth, yes." And he says, "Yeah, but your parents weren't *Nazis!*" I say nothing. He looks at me and leans forward in my typing chair and then says again, this time haltingly, "But your parents weren't *Nazis*, were they?" And I say, "Oh, Andy, look, this is all so . . . yes. They were." And as removed in time and tone his question has been from when it was asked of me for that very first time, as a sixteen-year-old exchange student, and as often as I have answered it since then, my heart contracts and I look past him as he says, in a low voice and with dismay, "Oh, no."

Always, I think, it will always be like that, as long as I live there will always be an equivalent of this bright and lovely twelve-year-old who has come to like me, who stands in line at the post office for me and at the photocopier's, who is enthralled by science fiction, draws elaborate and darkly funny cartoons, and keeps me up-to-date on which rock group is his favorite this month. There will always be someone like him, who will be aghast, saddened.

And there will always be Christian men—dolts, whose families have been in this country for generations—who will tell me, once they know the barest minimum about my parents, how "taken" they are, or were, with Hitler, the cautious ones merely with the "idea" of him, with "certain aspects"; men who presume to please me by delivering themselves of such information, assuming they are fashioning a common bond. ("It's a fact, after all. If the business with the Jews hadn't happened, he'd now be hailed as Germany's greatest leader.") While there may yet be another Jewish man whose interest in me translates into "fascination" with my "background." ("Was he a member of the Gestapo? Did he let you hold his gun? Did you like his boots? Would you like me to wear boots like that?")

The temptation, whenever I've moved from one job or place to another, to pronounce myself Swiss, or Swedish ("*Ingeborg*, that's Scandinavian, isn't it?") or Danish or Dutch—how many Americans would know the difference? Or to say, when the conversation comes around to it, that my father was a member of the Austrian underground, spent time in Nazi prisons, months in hiding . . . the last wouldn't even be a lie.

If I felt about Jews as I do about Norwegians—a complex and interesting people—then I could do it. And then there would be no need to do it. As it is, though, and having my flesh crawl at the sound of Yiddish, while my father was an SS man. . . .

To say, "My father was a Nazi," is bad enough. To say, "He belonged to the SS," and to say it in Manhattan, today, means that every listener assumes my father pushed bodies into gas chambers, spent quiet evenings stretching skin into lampshades.

Never mind that in 1938, as part of the *Anschluss*, all Austrian police officers were subsumed under the German police. Never mind that the head of the German police was Heinrich Himmler, whose title was Leader of the Police and SS of the Greater German Reich. Never mind that every single officer of the (former) Austrian police force automatically became a member of the SS, that the legion of cops, elevated to the ranks of the SS overnight, were not asked if such a rank was agreeable to them, or that they were not required to go to so much as a single indoctrination meeting.

No matter. In this country, now, SS stands for Death's-Head Battalion, means Extermination Camp Guard. One day my father was a cop—albeit a cop who fervently believed in Hitler and the *Anschluss*—playing in the Graz police band. Next day he was an SS man, playing in the Graz police band.

Had the idea appealed to him, there is no question that he would have joined that group years before. They would have been happy to have him. He was Aryan a certifiable five generations back, possessed of a head shape flawlessly conforming to Aryan ideals, had joined an underground activist cell as a very young man, and had been a member of the party for all the years it was illegal and dangerous in Austria to be a National Socialist. The SS would have considered him a perfect specimen for their "elite corps." Even their code, "My honor is loyalty," could have been invented by him.

But he had joined neither the SA nor the SS. Instead, the SS joined him.

Some months after Austria had become part of the Greater German Reich, my father was sent to Munich. His new superiors valued his long-standing party credentials, but he was still only a grammar school graduate and needed the equivalent of my *Matura* to qualify for advancement into police administration. "Police Administration" was a big step up for a street cop playing in a band.

My father was thrilled, at both the idea of advancement and the thought of being given a high school education. He started at thirty-three, a prudent age for a *Gymnasium* pupil. He was not surprised when he was pronounced good with numbers, and pleased to be told that he would end up not only a graduate but also an accountant, the furthest anyone in his family had progressed in terms of education and occupation.

A "Police Accountant"—can this be yet another specter? I write to a friend, a lawyer for the Austrian Ministry of Interior in Vienna, and ask: In what way could my father have been professionally involved with Jews? Could he have kept track of possessions taken from those who were being carted off, could he have noted in his ledgers who profited from such possessions? Could he have profited himself?

Throughout our *Gymnasium* career, my friend and I had the same history teacher, a slovenly, gentle woman who told us about the Stone Ages and the Phoenicians and the Middle Ages and the

Renaissance and right up to where Princip murders our Crown Prince. Then we went back to the Stone Ages again, in more detail.

If questioned about certain other chunks of history, our professor explained, "Your teachers and parents all lived through recent events. Recent events cannot be taught dispassionately. Therefore we do not teach recent events. We teach history. History does not allow for partisan views."

This professor held us captive with tales of numerous and obscure illnesses besetting her aunts. It was our version of soap opera, and we were more interested in the saga of these ailments than in either the Phoenicians or the pursuit of what was obviously a closed topic.

So my dear friend shares with me an appalling lack of "recent" historical knowledge, at least in terms of what had been handed down to us by the Austrian school system. However, her superior at the Ministry is better informed. He reviews my father's case and "considers it unlikely that there was any overlap whatsoever between your father's accounting responsibilities and the official, and top-secret, *Judenpolitik.*"

A different Austrian friend says, "What? When did you say he made inspector? Forty-four? How many Jews do you think were around for him to get rich off?"

Viewed as hard-core research it's not much; still, I let it go.

I have shown what I have written so far to a close friend. He says there are things he wants to talk about but he is exceptionally busy and why don't we have coffee in the morning before he goes to work. He lives nearby and we decide to meet at my house.

My friend can be blunt, one of the qualities I admire about him, and he is a Jew. He tells me he dislikes the "anti-Semitism segments."

When I had first told him I was to embark on this project I had also quoted a couple of my Christian friends to him. "Look, everybody feels like that, but you sure as hell don't talk or write about it." "You really want the Jewish Defense League demonstrating in front of your building?" "You've forgotten that ninety-nine percent of all New York publishers are Jews."

Back then this friend had said, "Just do it. If you ever want my opinion, I'll let you know when you're getting obnoxious."

Now he says, "Anti-Semitism is a *strong word*." And, "You are *not* an anti-Semite."

I try to recall pertinent passages, specific words. Hadn't I said, ". . . the taste in your mouth just before you throw up"? Hadn't I said, "seething," "revulsion"? Weren't there specific examples?

But my examples do not hold up for my friend. "Yiddish, you can't really count that, that's more of a purist reaction," he says. And, "The Hasids in the photograph, well, I might feel like that myself, and I'd call that a specifically American kind of uneasiness. We're all wary of an obvious unwillingness to assimilate." There is a pause. "Don't you see? You are overstating the case against yourself. You are not showing sufficient cause." And, one more time, "Anti-Semitism is a *strong word*. It may all be just a matter of language. Look, maybe you're not completely aware of what connotation that word has, in America."

I feel as dense as if I had just awakened from fourteen hours of drugged sleep. I ask a question, he reexplains his reservation, I ask the same question a second time, he patiently begins anew. Only gradually do I hear my questions become less feeble, more pointed. "Who *is* an anti-Semite?" "Where *is* the dividing line?" My friend continues to answer articulately and at length. And then at last his patience eludes him and he bursts out, as if driven against a wall, aloud, "But *Ingeborg*, don't you *understand*, an anti-Semite is *a terrible person!*"

He is fixed in my memory, hunched forward over empty coffee cups, Harvard-polished eloquence pared down to how he, Gerry Weinstein, feels. I think: He got up at seven to be here at eight, to have one piece of toast and to do his best to convince me, for the duration of three hours, that I am not what I am.

Can he be right? "With your particular background, someone who looks obviously Jewish is bound to arouse, say, *conflicting feelings* in you." Makes sense. And he's a *Jew!* If *he* doesn't think I'm an anti-Semite, who am *I* to quarrel with him? Maybe it is all "just a matter of language." Don't mention *anti-Semitism* then, don't say *prejudice*, just leave out those . . . words; follow the advice of this thoroughly decent person and declare yourself a woman who, because of her background, simply happens to have *conflicting feelings* about hats pushed off white foreheads.

But it is, after all, not true. What is true is merely that I do not tell "kike" jokes, do not live in an apartment building where Jews are less than welcome, do not join clubs that discourage memberships of certain ethnic groups. I do not voice what I feel. It would not occur to me to indulge in a habit comparable to that of one of my Jewish friends who, when a colleague of German parentage leaves the room, has been heard to hiss, *"Germans, Germans, how I hate Germans!"*

Yet though I haven't been to a church in years, I clearly remember the priest who prepared us for First Communion. "Evil thoughts are sinful, just as evil deeds are." Both were to be confessed. "I got really mad at my brother this week and kept thinking how I want him to go far away, Monsignor. Monsignor, I had envious thoughts about Gertrude next door, she always gets to stay outside even when it starts getting dark. This week I wanted to steal a jar of jam my mother made, to keep it just for me, Monsignor. . . ."

I do not voice what I feel—about whom? If there is no Jewish *person* toward whom I bear ill will, who or what else is there?

A colleague comes to my desk. "I'm collecting money for the Jewish . . ." She is talking rapidly and amiably, looking down at me in my chair. I look up at her equally amiably. She does not know that I have blanked out at the word "Jewish." I have become a mannequin in the position of a woman seated in an office swivel chair, face uplifted in an attitude of pleasing attentiveness. Inside me there is no thought, there is only a pulse that courses through me and says: No.

Within the mannequin, a registering process must have continued to function, it notes that the woman has stopped speaking. As if I were to say, "Oh, come to think of it, I don't have any manila ones either, I'll get an extra batch for you later," just like that, then, I say, "I'm sorry, you've caught me at a bad time, you're talking to the grand owner of one token and sixty-five cents. But I'm going to the bank in half an hour, why don't you stop by later."

"Great," she says and goes away.

I want to crawl under my desk. Instead, I snatch up my purse, smile at the woman at the desk next to mine, go to the washroom, and lock myself into a cubicle.

Slowly, methodically, I attempt to think. What did she ask me? To contribute money to a cause. What cause was it? I go over her words, but the words to go over are few. "I'm collecting money for the Jewish . . ." The Jewish what? Clearly, I did not want to know. Clearly, I also did not want to contribute. Aware of the odd sensation of sitting on a toilet while all my clothes are zipped and buttoned up, I count forty-seven dollars and change. It is an idle exercise since I knew all along, at least approximately, how much money I have in my wallet. I do not intend to go to the bank, the forty-seven dollars will last me until payday.

Why didn't I say, "I'm sorry, but I don't care to contribute to this . . . whatever"? Unthinkable. I cannot face what wells up in me at the idea of giving a dollar to a Jewish anything, I cannot face what causes me to undergo a sensation so powerful that I must, at all costs, erase it.

Eventually I go back to my desk, and eventually my colleague returns, and I smilingly hand her the dollar I have sitting ready, folded in half, next to my appointment book. She smiles back briefly, she's in a hurry, and checks me off her list and is on to the next desk. I find I have indeed run out of manila envelopes and walk to the supply closet only to stand before it, holding on to its opened metal doors, surveying the rows of pencils and erasers and boxes of paper clips, unable to remember what I have come to retrieve.

And that's it. I am out of examples.

While my Christian friends speak of feelings similar to mine—never, of course, in "mixed company"—most of them, too, misunderstand. They consider our *conflicting feelings* natural, "background" or no "background." "It's a bonding principle." "They're different, that's all, and sometimes it gets on your nerves." "You want to hear my father's definition of an anti-Semite? Somebody who hates Jews more than absolutely necessary." "It's that whole alien thing and old hat and boring as hell, but they're the ones who insist on it." "That bunch sticks together like glue, look around, one hand's always washing another." "But

God forbid *we* stick together, then it's no bonding principle anymore, hell no, then it's *prejudice*."

Yes, it is because of my "background" that I am more aware of how I feel about this particular—what; topic?—than any third-generation American-born Methodist friend of mine. My background, or my reaction to my background, does do that: makes me aware of "it." But "it," however unvoiced, however not-acted-upon, however unacknowledged, is anti-Semitism. The core of it. The germ of it. The kernel, the possibility, the essence of it. The necessary seed from which, in the proper environment, under the proper encouragement, with the proper nourishment, grows the thing that even officially cannot but be called by its true name. Whether it is the club that does not admit Jews—a little seedling there; or a university that limits the number of Jewish students it will accept—the seedling grows; or that same university refusing teaching positions to Jews—a sturdy little tree now; or a decree prohibiting Jews from using all public facilities—deep woods stretching into the distance; pogroms and a *Kristallnacht* and full-scale evacuation—unchecked growth in all directions at once, and no horizon in sight; until it's here, the jungle, dense and all-consuming, devouring a continent, its vines entangling a world.

I am sorry to disappoint you, Gerry, and any Jews who assume that all their Christian friends (none of whom, possibly, voice what they feel) are untainted by aspects of what you call, unfairly backed against the wall and with my very best interests at heart, being *a terrible person*.

So he studied to become a high school graduate and an accountant at the same time. And if the chief of police in this longed-for Greater Germany happened to also be chief of the SS, that's how it was. My father's new title had little bearing on what he now concentrated on with verve: Math and German Literature, with a special emphasis on Friedrich Schiller.

When all that was over, my father's cram course, his three-year career as Police Accountant culminating in the title of *Inspektor* on November 1, 1944, and ending in early May of 1945 with a stolen Jeep, a stolen horse, followed by months of hiding in haylofts;

when all that was over, and he started out again in a basement, making keys—that's when the telling of boyhood stories ended, that's when Friedrich Schiller invaded my life.

From the autumn of 1945 until the autumn of 1946, my father taught me *Das Lied von der Glocke*, "The Song of the Bell."

He would come home at night to his still-healthy wife, to his recuperating infant son, to his five-year-old daughter. He came home black with grease. Every time I've had a key made in this country, I have looked closely at the man who did the job for me, in a couple of minutes—in a shop, for instance, along an underground arcade at Grand Central. The man always wears jeans and some sort of shirt, clean, and his fingernails are no cleaner and no dirtier than those of a mailman, a bus driver, a teacher's aide; and I wonder what could have been so different about the work of a locksmith as performed by my father in 1945 and 1946 and 1947, from that of an American locksmith today.

My mother traded a blouse for a special cleaning solution and tried to invent solutions of her own, combining the granules labeled "laundry soap," available in exchange for coupons at grocery stores, with her mother's recipe for homemade soap, suitable for washing up after a day's work in the fields. But my father's hands no longer came clean. Even the lines on his forehead and around his nose and mouth remained for those years etched in dark, as if retouched by an inept photographer. For me, the perpetual grime under his fingernails and tracing every crevice of the hands folded in his lap, is ingrained in each stanza of Schiller's poem.

My very own father, green eyes vying with shiny, white teeth for splendor, his uniform taut across the back, tapering to a narrow waist; glittery, pretty things on chest and shoulders; a cap with its black visor, smooth, so that your fingers slipped across it as on ice, its band of leather lining matching in odor and touch the boots that reached above my waist . . . this man, my father, had been replaced by someone who walked with a stoop, who came home

173

black. The area surrounding the pupils of his eyes glowed pink.

Every night he spent half an hour cleaning himself as best he could, changed his clothes, and wolfed down whatever his wife had managed to concoct. Then he set me down in front of him, on the low kitchen stool, and taught me a few lines from memory, teacher and student driven by the same adrenaline. The grim stranger's urgency sped through me, inspiring a compliance so total that it informed a blazing urgency of my own.

Why was any poem, why was this poem, so important to him, to us? It was simple on my side. As odd as this type of attention was, nonetheless it was a set amount of time's worth, nightly, from a man whom I knew I was meant to accept as my new father. So memorize I did.

It may have been simple on his side, too. The "Bell" may have been the one poem they'd dealt with in detail, in Munich, when he was working toward his belated *Gymnasium* exams. But any old poem, even if studied in preparation for a high school exam come late in life—he was thirty-six when he "graduated"—does not move a man to replicate it on the brain cells of his small daughter, evening after evening, after he has put ten hours of manual work behind him and before he sets out to find that night's woman.

By the time I started first grade I had learned all twenty-nine stanzas, the longest one consisting of fifty-six lines. Did he think he would vanish, imminently, abruptly? Was *Das Lied von der Glocke* the one legacy he could think of worth leaving to this first-born? Schiller uses the physical construction of a church bell as a frame. Within this frame he follows the course of human life from infancy to death as seen from his early-nineteenth-century point of view; as seen, in fact, from a point of view narrow, if understandable, even for the early nineteenth century—couched though it is, particularly as my father used to recite it, in the most rousing, romantic, and beautiful language I expect to know.

"Do you talk much in bed?" "When you're in bed with someone, do you talk?" "Do you talk while you're . . . ?" I cannot get the phrase right, and it must be right before I ask him. I am in a daze, smiling at him fixedly and clutching a paper plate holding an untouched sandwich. We're at a reception at the Austrian Institute. He is speaking to me in German, with an Austrian accent so heady, so strong, so sweet, that I keep shivering in an overheated room. He may well be telling me where he buys his *Daily News,* all I hear is sounds.

Sanity prevails. I remind myself that is is unwise to make blatant if obscure propositions five minutes into a conversation, and refrain from asking my question. But for weeks I fantasize about having my body adorned with dripping Austrian vowels, being thrilled to ecstasy by consonants left unpronounced. I am unable to recall what he looked like. I only remember the lilts and slurs and graceful loops, the arches and bays: Austrian.

English, the language I have been using daily for nearly two decades, which I have taught my children and with which I earn my living, has always felt like one vast euphemism. "Shit" is what my friends and I say when we've run out of change in a pay phone, *Scheisse* shocks me. Only *Tragödie* sounds tragic; "tragedy" is made maudlin by its mushy *g*, weak by its brevity and lack of the long, heavy *ö*. "Hate," rhyming as it does with "Kate" and "great," is flaccid compared to *Hass*. "Longing" is nice, but *sehnen* . . . "Hail Victory," or "Victory Hail," either way, means nothing, is nothing. *Sieg Heil* rushes a chemical through my body, makes me react physically, and not only in disgust; it signals to an unencoded area. And there's *Jude*.

I look up "bigot" in the English-German section of my Cassell's dictionary. Four entries are given: *Frömmler, Eiferer, Fanatiker, blinder Anhänger.*

I look up each of these words in the German-English section of the same dictionary. A *Frömmler* is noted as a "hypocrite, devotee"; an *Eiferer* is a "zealot"; a *Fanatiker* is a "fanatic"; an *Anhänger* (*blinder* means "blind") is a "partisan, adherent; disciple, supporter; hanger-on." There's no bigot to be found.

A simple error in cross-referencing, possibly; but that is how irretrievably lost nuances get, not just minor ones either, all the time, in any translation.

Until I started on this book, which has led me to the Austrian consulate and its branches, I made it a point not to have acquaintances who were born where I was born. And on my visits to Austria a series of sensations repeats itself as if on a loop of film.

I am awash with sentimentality weeks before the trip, beside myself at the thought of going *home*, each time too excited to sleep on the plane. Then I'm there, Austria, Graz, where I belong. My surroundings are exquisite, the geraniums sheltering the sidewalk cafés are real, the food is beyond compare, I melt whenever I look at my brother, his family, my other relatives, my two or three remaining friends. Yet something is wrong. Either the place is wrong, or *I* am wrong, but something is tediously, odiously wrong. I get diarrhea, I speak only English to waiters and salespeople, I want everyone around me to be older than I am by the amount of years adults were older when I was growing up. People my own age scare me. Outside, I'm only comfortable at dawn, no one around. An old man washes down a sidewalk, then carefully sweeps excess water into the gutter. The sidewalk ends up clean enough to, well, to eat off.

A few hours later I must do an errand. I'm on a nearly empty side street, walking behind a small boy who is holding his mother's hand. For a moment he slips his hand out of hers, throws a candy wrapper into the gutter, reaches back up. The woman, she appears to be my age, slaps him. The boy looks to his right, his left, over his shoulder. He has blushed a bright red. He bends over quickly and retrieves the scrap of paper.

I am transfixed, thought piling madly onto thought. I'll run after them, I'll strew the contents of my pack of cigarettes on the sidewalk, I'll empty my handbag in front of the woman's shoes, I'll whisk off the boy, she will never see him again, first I'll knock her sprawling. . . .

"What are you making such a fuss over," says my brother tranquilly that same evening. "You don't know a thing about those two. They might have been shopping for three hours, both of them tired and cross. She may already have told him, nicely, six times in a row, not to throw trash on the ground, she may never have slapped him before, she may never slap him again, you're getting worked up over nothing."

But I want to be *home*, on my corner, on my block, watching a great, big slob throw his McDonald's wrapper on the sidewalk.

While I long for Austria when I'm here (sometimes seeing myself as an Austrian held captive in New York against her will) and while I can barely wait to leave Austria once I'm there (immediately feeling like a New Yorker stranded in Graz) there is one constant. Austria's language enchants me.

Grazerisch barely has the distinction of a specific accent, let alone a dialect like Carinthian or Styrian. The Viennese tend to go on a bit about their accent, consider it synonymous with Austrian, and the way they talk does charm me. But there is an edge to how people in my hometown transform German that sets it apart from what you hear in any other town or area in Austria.

How many Austrian dialects and accents are there—ten, twenty, forty, a hundred? Something to do with mountains separating valleys, people living in isolated villages for centuries, each valley, each village developing its own idiosyncrasies, and they continue to linger. All of them German, none of them German, all of them Austrian.

There is more to language than how it is spoken, though the sound itself is, of course, by far the most important part. There is the maddening fact, familiar to anyone who uses as the language of daily life one not inculcated first: you keep running into words, whole fragments, that cannot be rendered in your current language, you keep running up against the impossibility of ever transmuting, you are stuck with translation.

Sometimes you don't even have access to that. It is impossible to express *dein verliebter Mund* in tolerable English. I tried once, it's a phrase out of the "Lilli Marlen" song. The lyrics to that song exist in English, but not that phrase, and I like that phrase very much. I worked at it, a challenge, but to no avail. "What a lovely concept," said my friend when I had finished trying to circumscribe the phrase by way of clumsy exposition. "It's about this idea, how when you're in love, your mouth—just by the way it looks— demonstrates to your lover that you are, in fact, in love. It means 'your In-Love-Mouth.'" But such gyrations, at best, only add up to "a lovely concept."

If English has always seemed to me like a collection of words somehow less strong, less specific, less direct, less moving than a second group of words, lately there has been a change. English is becoming a digital code; it serves.

This change is a loss to me and I mourn it. I clearly remember loving English, truly loving fragments of a sentence, whole paragraphs, euphemism they may be, feel them shine! A long list of favorites, from Elizabeth Jane Howard calling cats "those artists of position," to Yeats's "the rag and bone shop of the heart."

German is turning into more than a means. German, transformed from polished brass into gold through the alchemy of tone, cadence, and melody, *my* German, Austrian, is turning into reality. Most meaning beyond information and all beauty are turning their back on English, taking up residence in my *real* language, beckoning me.

I fight it. I didn't just learn English to find my way around a foreign country, I had more at stake than that. Lose that accent, get that intonation! Working at a magazine, earning the reputation of being good at "line-by-line" editing, having the skill to manipulate small fragments of this foreign language, improving on a sentence written by a native, under the spell of the illusion that such a skill might, somehow, eventually, make me a native too.

But I could not write about my parents or my childhood in German. My knight in shining armor, my saving-grace shield, is English.

An eminent Jewish author is being interviewed on television. I have long admired this writer's work. He is wearing a dark green suit that looks to be made of velvet, his handsome, sharp-featured face more like a Frenchman's than a Central European's. "How do you explain," asks the interviewer off-camera, "I mean, how do you think it was possible that human beings could have committed such unspeakable crimes?"

The man on whom the camera is focused thinks, and thinks some more, and the camera and I reverently watch him think. Finally he says, "I don't understand the victims, and I don't understand the killers. But the victims are my problem, and the killers are yours."

An ache bites into my brain, squarely at the back of my head. It is severe enough for me to be careful, for the moment, not to move. Being hit over the head, I think, that's what that phrase means, it's not figurative at all. By the time I find the bottle of aspirin, the television voices have receded into static. I drink some water from my toothbrush tumbler and think, An articulate man. One aspirin sticks in my throat. A truly articulate man. I gulp more water, then some milk. And he has a point, too. The aspirins do nothing for my head (not yet; a matter of waiting fifteen, twenty minutes) while thought—beyond "articulate" and ". . . a point" —has deserted me. Only gradually do I become aware of something moving in me, a thing below thought, a thing uncoiling, hot and poison-bitter and beyond aspirin, confession, and general anesthesia alike: Ah, for such decisive, facile cutting adrift of the other side, such clear-cut division of who is whose problem. How determinedly, how slowly, with what sober finality he presented this conclusion of his, which clearly holds for him. And how I yearn to be able to say what he says, just turn it around, this thesis, this epigram, this pronouncement, grim as it sounds: "The victims are your problem. Only the killers are mine." But this way around the epigram falls apart. Too much is left out, far too many are cut off.

Then the headache is forgotten because the pain inside me swamps to the surface and there's a shape to it, and this is it: All *right*, Eminent Jewish Author! Or rather: Thank *you*, Eminent Jewish Author! I'll try it your way. What *do* I know about the victims, come to think of it, those legions who haunt me? Not a solitary thing beyond what I've read, in this writer's work and many others', along with a few photographs of massed naked bodies, seen so often they have transmuted into icons.

But the killers, the *killers*, the "killers"—those I haven't just read about, some of those I know.

And I know this: I'm not a killer.

And I know this too, and just as well: Neither my father nor my mother was a killer, even if (here in my self-styled homeland Manhattan) among most of the people I know, my Nazi parents are lumped as such, by automatic implication, unselfconsciously, by common consensus, as a matter of course.

So enough, then. Enough of that automatic breast-beating, this eternal leaning-over-backward, every thought of my childhood, my family, my country, my heritage warped forever. Except that taking this on—unsure even of what "this" is—scares and exhausts me into sleepless nights, into reckless experiments with oblivion, into relentless disgust with the effort not to just let it all be, to draw instead on what's buried inside me, covered solidly as with damp earth, a forever-new grave under thin rain.

I spent much of the last two years of the war on my grandparents'
farm. A few times my parents miscalculated the timing of one of
my visits home, and Graz was bombed while I was in town. There
were sirens, there was running, there were frightened adults, later
dead bodies or parts of bodies, and walls that looked like the back
wall of a dollhouse. You could tell where a room used to end and
where another had once begun. Next to a patch of dark green
would be a light blue one, a border of flowers near the top; or a
whole square of gold arabesques; or a stretch painted white, not a

smudge from the lick of a flame, dark roses on pink, pretty dollhouses four stories high.

My parents had not succeeded in sheltering me so completely as they would have liked. There had been the smell and sight of the woman still alive, though burning brightly; two neighbors had tried to pull her out from under rubble, they had beaten at the flames and tugged hard, but they had not been able to move her in time. I had seen other such casualties, not many, but some. None had given me nightmares.

Only now, though it was nearly summer and I could watch the shadows of clouds move across the valley below like ships, though my mother and baby brother were with me and all bombs had stopped, now I screamed at night.

I knew, though no one had spoken a word of it to me, that something had come to an end. The turning point had been precise. I had been home for the first time in a very long while, all four of us had left Graz at once, there had been a boy.

In early May 1945, my father abandoned his ledgers and stole a Jeep parked in front of police headquarters. Its tank, miraculously, was a quarter full, at a time when all of Greater Germany had been out of gasoline for weeks. He collected his wife and daughter at the apartment and his gravely ill son at the hospital, picking him up out of a crib over the mechanical protest of a sleepwalking nurse in charge of row after row of children. And he put his son on my mother's lap. She sat next to her husband, and I sat in back next to a couple of suitcases, a cardboard box held together with string, and the wall clock my mother had bought a week after her wedding.

He drove rapidly through the streets of Graz and then more slowly over country roads, amid people pushing loaded bicycles or pulling handcarts, all of them going in our direction. Even later we rode steeply uphill, the occasional hollows in the dirt road filled in with halved tree trunks, making the road passable for ox carts after heavy rain. The sky cut a swath into the pines that thickened, three rows deep at either side of us, into dense forest.

We have seen no one for a while but now there is a boy, just ahead of us. He balances on one of the lengths of wood embedded in the ground and waves, holding something in his waving hand. My father brakes sharply and makes a convulsive movement with both arms, arching them above his head and toward the woods, shouting. The boy waves once more and then stops, his arm in midair. His right hand is gone. "Lucky kid," a physician friend has said to me. "I would have thought a grenade could do more damage than just blowing off a hand." The same friend has insisted that my memory deceives me. "It isn't possible," he said. "The blood spurts out a fraction of a second later. Imagine all those severed veins. . . ." But, possible or not, I see—arranged within the stump—the circular ends of something like small, cut-off, white straws. That's what I see first.

My father takes one of the two blankets belonging to a Graz children's hospital off his son on my mother's lap and walks toward the boy who stands rigid and still, his right arm raised in what seems a familiar gesture. My father winds the blanket around the wrist, which the boy continues to hold at what is a convenient height for my father's efforts. When he gets to the end of the blanket my father seems, for a moment, at a loss. As soon as he has tucked the fabric in place, it falls away again and begins to unwind. But he tears into the blanket with his teeth and produces strips of cloth, which he ties around the bulk of the blanket already in place on the boy's forearm.

189

"You'll be all right now," my father says, "you are coming with us." The boy does not move. My father carries him to the Jeep, repeating what he has already said, slightly varying the sequence of words. "You're okay," "We've got plenty of room," "You'll be all right now; you're coming with us."

My father asks me to get up, stacks the suitcases and the cardboard box on the floor, tells me to sit down again, and lays the clock on my lap. He has to force the boy's legs at the knees to get him to sit down beside me. The boy is older than I am, maybe old enough to go to school, his hair is brown, his nose is white. He looks straight ahead. From the corner of my eyes I watch the pale gray blanket darken, an even seeping, fast and sly as magic.

When my father tries to restart the Jeep it sputters, falters, makes one last, small jump. The boy turns his head toward and past me, abruptly faces forward again, jumps off his seat and runs into the woods. That's when we all started walking. My father took the cardboard box under one arm and a suitcase in each hand, the clock stayed behind, and we saw neither clock nor Jeep again. My mother carried my brother, whose eyes were closed and who lay silent throughout the afternoon's journey. Off and on, my mother stopped walking and held her ear close to the baby's mouth.

As soon as we were within sight of my grandparents' farm, my father set down box and suitcases and started back downhill. My mother and brother and I were safe. As my mother told me later that evening, it was considered unlikely that any army would climb our mountain in order to conquer isolated farms one by one.

My father walked for a few hours—it was dark by then—until he came upon a horse in a field just off the road. For the next eight hours he rode this horse across Styria, avoiding towns and villages, always in the direction of artillery fire, which was also the direction in which his mother's village lay. I assume he had at least a policeman's pistol (did police accountants routinely carry guns?) since I cannot imagine how else he thought he would defend himself or anyone else against the soldiers of an enemy army. I do know he was wearing civilian clothes, the first time I remember seeing him out of uniform. (Reality was different, as a photograph of him in civilian clothes with me on his lap clearly proves.)

He stayed up for what was left of the night and the next day, while his mother and sisters hid. But the Russians did not, after all, come directly through the village in which he grew up. They went through Judenburg instead, not far away. The father of the girl who eventually married my brother was killed there, one day before the end of the war.

I do not remember a doctor ever visiting the farm, or that my sick brother was taken down to the village. My grandmother made teas for him out of herbs she had spread to dry on the attic floors, but his fever continued.

During the day I was fine. I was used to being by myself among adults who got up at five and went to bed at midnight. Since both sons had been drafted, and since the man I called Grandfather was old and tired easily, the farm was run by Aunt Zenzi and my grandmother, assisted by two fieldhands exempted from military service. Hans was unstable and twice a week drunk, the other one a retarded midget whose eyes skipped helplessly from side to side.

There were cows to be fed and milked, there was a horse, there were pigs and sheep, there was a vegetable garden, there were the fields, too steep for machinery. The men sowed in wide sweeps, later on they mowed in the same motion. When they stopped to sharpen their blades, and if the sun hit the metal just right, the scythes seared the air as half-moons of lightning. The women tied sheaves of rye into bundles and piled them onto ox carts and drove them up the steep incline to the farm. They smoked the meat from home-slaughtered animals, baked all the bread, cooked all the meals, washed everyone's laundry at the well. My aunt skimmed each day's milk of cream until there was enough to pour into a wooden drum on legs, a peg on one side of the drum serving as the handle with which to keep the drum in motion. I turned the wheel.

You hold on to the handle and pull it up, letting gravity make it fall, pulling it up again, down. When your arm is numb you switch arms, when your other arm is numb you switch back. Inside the drum the cream makes a rhythmic, sloshing noise. When you have given up hope, this noise stops, you hear a triumphant thump instead, you have made liquid into a firm clump of butter, beads of moisture clinging to its surface, a marvel for all to see.

Water was carried in from the well. Slivovitz was home brewed, the bottles guarded against Hans in Grandfather's special cellar. The women planted and harvested flax and spun it into thread and wove it into linen and sewed that into sheets and curtains and shirts and towels. They sheared sheep, washed the wool, spread it on grass to bleach in the sun, spun it, and knitted it into sweaters and underwear and scarves and heavy caps.

Cooking was done on a wood-burning stove. Two men at either end of a saw cut down trees and spent weeks hacking them into pieces, one hatchet to a man. The kitchen stove was the farm's one source of heat. Electricity was installed in 1977. Now there is a freezer to keep meat fresh without salt, no television yet but a radio.

Aunt Zenzi's husband shows me around. He points out the new purchase for the stable: upon receiving a small electric shock, the cows keep clear of the shallow trough just below their hind ends. Water, channeled from the well outside, gushes through the trough.

My aunt looks pleased while her husband demonstrates the new system. This man has made her happy, though she had child after child in the middle of winter, when neither doctor nor midwife could get through the snow. The last one had presented complications. Weeks after the delivery Zenzi was brought to Graz, deathly ill; after surgery she recovered with us. She had been the most-sought-after woman of the region in her youth, traces of her beauty are still unmistakable. Now she looks at her husband with a hint of amusement while he explains, "It was indoor plumbing this year or the irrigation system. The girls complained, but what do they know? All those years I've spent cleaning out manure with a shovel and my two hands. Next year, I tell them, it'll be indoor plumbing next year."

Back then, when I wasn't a "visitor from America" but a four-year-old native, a bunch of wasps once built a nest in the outhouse. Their buzz sounded like a thousand threats to me, I dared not move when stray ones settled on my hair. Only one of the adults noticed that I began to bypass the outhouse to take short walks in the forest behind the farm.

The man I called Grandfather talked even less than the others. It seems improbable to me now that he should have said nothing, year in, year out, beyond his version of "Our Father" (only the first two words and the Amen intelligible, the rest a quick and soothing blur), but I do not remember him saying anything else. That the old man had preferred hunting to farming all his life may have given him an edge on observation. One afternoon he motioned me to follow him to the outhouse, then to stay back at a distance. He wore the net bonnet he used when tending to his stock of bees, and flailed his hand-carved walking stick.

Having the outhouse back was solid comfort. For one thing, its door could be shut with a sliding bolt. For another, there was a wood bench to sit on, high for me, but preferable to squatting on pine needles, ants crawling over my bare toes. Happy to be back in this small, secure place (now only thick with flies; old Church bulletins torn into squares and stacked neatly in a corner), happy and at my most daring, I stuck my head into the round hole. I wanted to see how far down it went, what it looked like down there, and what it might be like to be down there.

Earlier that day I had asked my mother why we prayed before meals here; we did not pray in Graz. "It reminds us to be good," she had said. "If we forget to be good we go to Hell, far, far below." And though I continue to be grateful to the man I called Grandfather, his thoughtfulness and my resulting research did saddle me with a theological reference peculiarly my own, which was to haunt me for years.

Rousting the wasps was not his only gift to me. One morning he beckoned with a forefinger and went outside. He led the way across the yard and stopped where the hayloft and stable adjoin at a right angle, forming an open niche covered by a wooden roof. He grinned below his drooping mustache, patterned after the one worn by the later Emperor, and pointed to a contraption not seen on the farm before. A set of ropes hung from the roof; a hole had been drilled into each end of a board. I had only recently learned the name of this wood from Hans. He had been at the talkative, not yet the violent stage, and had recited the names of woods for me: birch and walnut, linden and willow, and something called *Sandelholz*, which a sailor friend had described to him, a kind of wood Hans did not expect but longed to see. This board was pine, its surface sanded to satin. The ropes had been threaded through the holes; sturdy knots supported the board at just the right height for me to sit on. He gave me the gentlest little push.

My mother's real mother, the woman who had abandoned her daughter and had not reclaimed her, did not talk much either; except for Hans, twice weekly, the adults around me went through their days nearly mute. All those years ago, had that been her decision? Letting the past rest, moving to a different province, starting a new life? Or had the decision been Grandfather's, a condition, a choice to be made. "Will you hang on to your bastard, who is being taken care of already, or will you marry me, have *my* children?"

Except for the times when she clucked at her chickens, my grandmother seemed remote to me and cold. This changed, and because of an enemy soldier. She let me feed the chickens with her from then on, sometimes she patted my head.

In their scramble for the cave they left my grandmother and me behind. My grandmother had stayed by choice. She was bent over from decades of farmwork and her face was no less weather-beaten than it would be twenty years later; anyone not from a farm like hers would assume her to be a frail old woman, and she felt safe behind her misleading appearance.

They did not find me in time to take me along. A four-year-old on a farm could be playing in a dozen different places, and it was crucial for the two younger women—my mother and Aunt Zenzi, who carried my brother—to reach the cave. The fieldhands trotted behind them, and Grandfather followed last, carrying his two most reliable rifles. The men hid because they expected an approaching enemy army to take even old and half-witted men prisoner. The women hid as women of a defeated country hide at the approach of a victorious army. Years later my mother told me how they had assured each other that I was cautious enough not to allow myself to be seen by uninvited strangers, which was true, and young enough (just as my grandmother considered herself old enough) to be of no interest to enemy soldiers, which was less true, as Austrians were to find out. The civilian population of those European countries taken over by the Russians for keeps would find out, in addition, that men can remain alive for two days while being roasted on a spit over an open fire, while death comes more slowly to naked women nailed through their palms to the side of a barn. But at the time, one did not yet conceive of such occurrences.

It was a clear day. From the kitchen window my grandmother saw what her husband had seen from a lookout point above the farm, earlier. The Russians were coming, there was the first one. My grandmother watched him trudge up the steep path, plod through the yard, stop at the water trough, and yank off his helmet. When he tilted his head and held his open mouth under the stream of water, she saw that he was at most eighteen, the age her youngest had been five years ago, the boy who had gone from being a shy and graceless child to being a shy and graceless recruit to being blown into pieces two weeks and one day into the war. The same hair, a dull blond that turns muddy gray when dirty and translucent gray when wet, only to brighten again into a flat yellow without a hint of gloss.

When he looked up from the well he saw her. He pulled the helmet down over his wet forehead and walked up the stone steps like a man twice his age and bulk. The dog barked but did not impede the soldier's progress, marking it instead, jumping up at him once on every step, its front paws on the young man's chest, gleeful.

He motioned my grandmother aside with his rifle and preceded her into the kitchen, speaking in what seemed an official tone. She shook her head. He unleashed a row of growls and she shrugged and shook her head again.

His rifle at the ready he searched the house. A lunge into the grandparents' bedroom and a running leap into the room holding sacks of grain, spinning wheels, and a loom seemed to reassure him; he mounted the staircase at the end of the hallway almost leisurely. Upstairs, he can only have taken a glance at the small bedrooms and the open area where old tools stood against sloping walls and the fieldhand straw sacks lay on the floor in each of the far corners. He lumbered downstairs again and did not notice me, cowering underneath the staircase against the stone wall, next to an exhausted cat giving birth to the last of a litter of seven.

Back in the kitchen he leaned his rifle against the wall, dropped his backpack onto the floor, and threw his helmet on the large, scrubbed-white wooden table with a clatter. He shaped his left hand into a shallow bowl, held it below his mouth, and made spooning motions with his right. His eyes, their lower halves white, were raised at the woman standing across from him, while his neck was bent forward sharply at the angle of a dog's. Neither of the adults noticed me. I had crept from under the stairwell toward the kitchen and crouched, concealed behind a stack of wood, next to the stove.

My grandmother took an egg from a basket at her feet. I had collected them earlier; there had been thirteen. She held up the egg and the soldier nodded and thrust up both hands, fingers spread into fans. "Ten!" said my grandmother sharply. "Nobody eats ten eggs in my house, not even a Russian." She took a second egg from the basket and held both aloft, then three, next four, two each poised precariously in either palm. The soldier stood with his legs spread wide, splayed fingers above his head, grinning broadly.

When she continued to display only four eggs while shaking her head, he dropped his arms. With three steps he was at her side, plucked at the basket, strode back to the table. A fawn-brown ivory-speckled egg, a slender piece of straw stuck to its side, wobbled gently on the tabletop. Snatching up his rifle and walking rapidly backward, the soldier put as much distance between himself and the table as the room allowed before aiming briefly, crouched low.

The effect of the blast was mystery. No fragments of shell were to be seen, no oozing yolk, no smears of transparent white anywhere, the egg had vanished. The soldier advanced on my grandmother, who laid the four eggs she had been holding into a pan at the back of the stove and covered her face with her arms. But he slung the rifle over his shoulder, merely picked up the basket of eggs, gathered the hem of her apron into his fist and carefully set eight eggs into the hollow. He dropped the empty basket, retrieved two more eggs from the pan, added them to the eight others, curled my grandmother's right hand around the gathered folds of fabric, and, grinning, repeated his gesture of one cupped hand below his chin, the other shoveling rapidly.

My grandmother knelt down before him. Without looking up, she transferred the eggs in her apron back into the basket. The soldier took the rifle off his shoulder once more and aimed at my grandmother's forehead. She rolled her eyes to the ceiling, drew one corner of her mouth far into the cheek beside it, and laid one hand flat on top of the unheated stove—now at the height of her chin—while pointing at the wood stacked next to the stove with the other.

He failed to grasp her meaning. He took one more step, so that the gun touched the skin between my grandmother's eyes. She thwacked the stovetop with her flat hand, then tapped a sharp forefinger to her temple twice, before pointing at him. The soldier looked from the cold stove to the old woman, back to the stove, and then at the wood. He broke into guffaws, returned to the table, carelessly dropped his rifle and sat down on a bench, his legs stretched into the room.

My grandmother stoked the stove and lit the kindling. Then she dragged a chair across the floor and sat down, a distance from the intruder. They both watched the stove while I watched them. I knew that my grandmother had seen me while preparing the fire and I felt calmed by this knowledge.

Not much later she set a frying pan onto the stove, slid lard off a knife into the pan, and broke ten eggs into the melted lard, setting the shells aside in a neat row. After some stirring she heaped the contents of the pan into a bowl, which she set onto the table along with the heel of a loaf of bread, a jug of home-pressed cider, and an enameled tin mug.

The soldier's face, a ridge from the helmet still embedded in his forehead, looked tired, but he pivoted sharply on his seat, set his boots down loudly under the table, and bent over the bowl. My grandmother sat down on the far end of the same bench, with her back to the table. She faced in the direction of my hiding place while watching the soldier out of the corner of her eyes.

When he was halfway through his meal she took her youngest son's induction photograph off the wall at arm's reach to her right, and held it toward the boy. He looked up, nodded, and drank the rest of his cider. She refilled his mug and pointed at the photograph, at the cider-drinking soldier, at his gun on the floor. Then she cocked one arm and stretched out the other, pretending to hold a rifle herself, and imitated gunshot sounds. They were louder than any noise I had heard my grandmother make.

The volley ended abruptly. She threw up her arms and fell back, her head hitting the table with a thud, her eyes shut, her mouth open. An instant later she jumped up again, her arms positioned once more as if holding a gun, her throat breaking into explosions, arms flailing, the collapse against the table more vehement than before. I covered my mouth. When my grandmother began to shoot a third time, the soldier, who had been watching her poses openmouthed, looked over his shoulder and once all around the room and then put his hand on my grandmother's arm. She sat up immediately and calmly pointed once more at the soldier, at his gun, and at the photograph of my dead uncle.

This time he studied the photograph at length before looking up at her and nodding several times. He watched her turn away from him and hang the picture on its nail, quickly and askew. Then he bent down again over his meal and finished the second mug of cider. Eventually he pushed away the bowl, still one-quarter full, and put his arms onto the table and his head down on his arms.

As soon as he had begun to breathe regularly, my grandmother motioned in my direction. Together we ate the lukewarm eggs. "Such a waste," she whispered, "wasting food like this." We wiped the bowl clean with crusts of bread, and I crept back to the woodpile without having to be told.

After what seemed a long time, my grandmother edged down the bench toward the sleeping soldier until they sat side by side. The boy shifted his weight several times, his face nearly touched her arm. My grandmother continued to look across his head at the windowless wall behind the stove. The dog, stretched flat beneath the table, twitched its tail at circling flies, the soldier snoring faintly now, his hair dry again and a flat yellow.

Something startled him later, it was almost dark, and he grabbed his rifle and helmet and ran down the steps outside the house and down the path between the fields.

It turned out that a Russian regiment had passed through, much farther south, and a few soldiers had become separated from the rest on their long march through the woods. There was little to laugh at that summer, and the lost Russian became a joke on farms as far away as the next province.

My father had disappeared, "in the countryside," as my mother put it. She would light the oil lamp and hold my hand, but neither she nor anyone else asked me why I screamed, night after night. Whatever had occurred remained nameless. Just as none of the adults around me had discussed the war during its duration—not, at any rate, in front of me—none of them bothered to mention that it was over. If they spoke at all, they might briefly remark on the waning health of a cow, or comment on which one among them would be missed least during the next day's work; someone had to walk the two hours to the village to buy salt, the one item that kept the farm from being self-sufficient. When I asked my grandmother whether my father was dead and would the rest of us die too, she replied, "I'm beginning to think that the brown-speckled hen has switched to laying at the far end of the hayloft," the longest sentence I have ever heard her say.

By the autumn of 1945 we were back in Graz, my brother was well, and a man who passed himself off as my father—not a policeman but a locksmith whom, it seemed, I could please by learning a poem—was part of our lives.

Since we returned to live in our old apartment (not by ourselves, of course, there were the Lehmanns; still, our address, available to anyone who might have cared, continued to be *Polizeisiedlung* 56) and since no one ever interrogated or pursued my father, I have wondered why he bothered to hide at all. It is only from relatives' guarded references that I have come to assume that the manner—

whatever it was—in which he spent much of the summer of 1945 may not have been prompted by internal reasons, known only to him, alone.

"Armed bands were roving the streets, things were in flux," says an aunt.

"If the cop in the apartment next door had been keeping his radio on 'high,'" says one of my uncles, "well, now you had a chance to get even. Denouncing an SS man was easy." The edge in his calm voice—*topic closed; over and out*—is as familiar to me as the slant of my hipbone.

A different uncle smiles, lights yet another Camel, and says, "Maybe he just didn't want to talk to anybody for a while."

"Why Camels?" I ask.

He tells me he came to like them as a prisoner of war. "The Americans weren't brutes, you understand, there just wasn't any food, some shipments had gone wrong, the guards were short on rations themselves. But thanks to an American Ladies' Club, the camp was knee-deep in Camels. Until the food started trickling in, they let us chain-smoke all day long."

All around us that fall, two families were settling into one apartment. The identical layout of these apartments prompted dozens of families to divide the available space identically, in the manner that made most sense for all concerned.

The front door opened onto a narrow, L-shaped hallway, ending at the toilet door. To the left of the toilet was a bathroom, containing a sink and tub. Also off the short arm of the L was a small room; my brother and I had slept in that. First off the long arm of the L had been my parents' bedroom, next to it my father's study; last—or first, as you came in the front door— was the living room, across from that the kitchen.

All around us, then, families decided to split the number of bedrooms between them, and to use such facilities as did not lend themselves to division—kitchen, bath, toilet—communally.

My father, granting up front that there was nothing to be done about the toilet, proceeded to tell the astonished Lehmanns that two families, forced to cook and eat in a single kitchen, would slay one another, and soon. He was short with words, black with grime, grim-faced. The Lehmanns saw his point. My father converted the bathroom into a makeshift kitchen and gave them a choice. Did they want to take the larger kitchen and walk through our side each time they went to the toilet? Or would they prefer to have the toilet on their side, make do with the smaller kitchen, and be obliged to walk through our half of the apartment when going out or coming home? They wisely chose to stick close to the toilet.

My father built a crude but solid door and installed it across the hallway. All eight of us—the two Lehmann boys paralleled my brother's age and mine—washed at our respective kitchen sinks. I soon remembered the original apartment only dimly.

It was early in the morning, nearly dawn, a year ago now, almost spring, I had worked thirty-two hours in a row, one day sliding into the next, I was utterly exhausted, I needed to go to sleep.

But not yet.

I had discovered that if I exhausted myself beyond a limit (its location in time was always elusive and unpredictable, yet precise once I had transgressed it) I could enter a landscape of sensation unlike any I knew.

There was emptiness. But there was also clarity, a fierceness of vision, the white of a piece of paper and the black of my typewriter engaged in so luminous a contrast that the page before me appeared as if rimmed by a halo.

There was the urge to sleep, which translated into the kind of ache associated with an ordinary flu. But what mattered was only what I was able to tell myself, then, and that I was able to convert what I was able to tell myself, then, into pitch-black letters on paper so bright it dazzled. There was no "thinking." All I did was feel. Full-time. Soon I'd be asleep. But before falling asleep, and for a short while only, I was afforded a glimpse worth staying awake for, beyond sense and reason. All other times my censors were far too efficient. They stomped out danger before it had the chance even to throw its shadow around a corner of my brain.

I felt: The legacy of the Holocaust has destroyed my father. I felt: The legacy of the Holocaust has irreparably damaged my mother's life. I felt: The legacy of the Holocaust has tarnished me beyond all methods of cleansing. I felt: I hate the guts of every Jew alive.

There was a typing error in each word by then, but I could not quite yet give in and lie down and drop off. When I'd wake up, I would, once again, disavow every word of this, possibly it would all be illegible, I had already done one paragraph with each of my fingers shifted over by one key. But I had to write about this then, while all my defenses had folded up their tents, while my ever-present censors had nodded off ahead of me, *then*, while the computer had shifted into downtime. What was awake and ablaze was a moonscape unsullied by logic, fairness, civilization.

I knew all about my *conflicting feelings* then, my anti-Semitism, and this was it: "The memory of . . . no, they can't take that away from me."

It was simple. If I detested anti-Semitism with my brain and soul, I had to distance myself from my parents to a degree unbearable for me. So I detested anti-Semitism with my brain alone.

In a crib-shaped recess within me, a child so small that it had yet to cross over into the kingdom of language had aligned itself with its almighty, adored parents; aligned itself with, and taken in, all whispers and shapes, all tastes, all silences, hums and glances, all colors, melodies, gestures and scents, lavished by these parents on their child; had taken them in, and on. A child holding hands, having its hands held; one small hand encircled by the large, warm hand of one parent, a second small hand enfolded in the large, warm hand of the other parent. A permanent allegiance, the most primitive holding-on—detestable, horrendous, pick the synonym of your choice—which linked me to my dead parents, to their dead parents, to their dead grandparents.

Had I no better links than this? Yes, and many. But anti-Semitism was one.

"It's up to you," I said, out loud. "If you want to be free of all that, you'd be free of your parents, too." But I did not want to be free of my parents. I did not. I did not, please, not that, I did not. Had I not observed every decency anyone, myself included, could possibly expect of me? Not a trace of an anti-Semitic slur out of me, ever, I neither spoke evil nor did I tolerate hearing it, my secret ballast hurt no one but me, it had become impossible to type, it was time to go to bed.

From the summer of 1947 through the autumn of 1950 my mother was confined to bed with a chronic kidney infection. At first, different relatives took in my brother and me. But I was no longer the amenable toddler who had seemed, on the whole, unscathed by new surroundings. Now, being away from home made me relentlessly weepy, a bother. Ernsti was as cheerful as I was sour, a little charmer, all were agreed on that. But he was extraordinarily curious as well, mischievous, reckless, and impossible to keep track of. Soon, both of us ended up back home. My father bought groceries during his lunch break, cooked for us all at night, and washed clothes and staircases. After some months it became too much for him. From then on, and until my mother was well, my parents employed a series of maids.

This idea had at first been rejected, not because of a maid's salary (which barely bought the stamps for her letters home) but because a maid needed room and board. "Board" was difficult, "room" seemed impossible. My brother and I had been sleeping in what had once been my father's study, my parents in the adjoining former living room, now my mother's sickroom as well.

What had once been my father's study, and more recently my brother's room and mine, now became the maid's. Ernsti's crib was pushed up against the footboards of my parents' double beds. I, at least in theory, slept between my parents, on a blanket that had been stuffed into the narrow gap separating their mattresses. In practice, this blanket formed a slight ridge, causing me to roll down into one or the other of the two beds just before I fell asleep. I liked alternating between my two valleys.

The maids were seventeen or eighteen, girls off a farm, their first time away from home. They had, of course, done housework for years, but they had not washed dishes under running water or cooked with electricity. My supine mother, who had once been such a girl herself, taught them how to make beds with mattresses instead of straw sacks, how to do the laundry, what to look for while selecting the daily groceries, and how to prepare those groceries to her specifications. She was sometimes in severe pain and always uncomfortable, she was bitterly unhappy over her enforced and seemingly endless immobility, she was in her mid-thirties and had not been ill before.

Every few weeks or months I watched my mother cry, a maid leave, a new one arrive, and my mother cry, and that maid leave. One, with brown hair and dark eyes, broke a plate. My mother scolded her. The girl took the money she had in an envelope, what was left of the train fare she had been given to get to our house, and bought—perhaps defiantly—the most beautiful plate she could find, small roses along a gold-rimmed border. My mother scolded her again, probably out of helplessness. She surely knew long before I did that her husband was sleeping with this one, too. The maid cried.

I am about to walk into the kitchen in my stocking feet. The door is only leaning against the frame, it opens quietly. Without crossing the threshold I can see the coat rack against the wall, three hooks at the top for hats, a mirror below the hooks, and a small drawer at the height of adults' waists that holds our family's odds and ends: bobby pins, thumbtacks, a crumpled bank note with many zeros, shoestrings. The maid stands before the mirror, her cheeks are wet and puffy, she is combing her hair. My father stands behind her. His left hand is on her shoulder, close to her neck, his right hand touches her hand that holds the comb. Its pointed teeth are poised in midair.

I was unable to go to sleep that night. My father, who most often went out, had stayed at home. He was reading the paper in the kitchen. I turned off the bedroom light, said good night to my mother, and settled down on my ridge. After some time there was the sound of the kitchen door being opened and closed, his five steps down the hallway—no tiptoes—and the opening and closing of the maid's-room door. My brother let out a small cry in his sleep, and my mother and I started in unison. I remembered what I had learned playing hide-and-seek. When the child who is looking for you has ventured close to your hiding place, and the thrill of the game makes a deafening, rushing-water noise in your ears, you breathe through your mouth; this makes your own breath inaudible, clears your head of inner noise, and sharpens your hearing. As soon as I began to breathe this way, I realized that my mother was doing the same. Together we listened to the sounds made by my father, the maid, and their bed.

Until my mother was well (the maids, if not yet my father's affairs, came to an end; their room and bed became mine), I stayed awake until he had gone to sleep. That he always returned to his bed for this purpose is cause for gratitude; had he made a habit of staying out all night, I might have slept through third and fourth grade.

I did not roll down my ridge into his bed again, and I refused to eat in the kitchen with my brother, the maid, and him. Furious that a child would pass up food he worked very hard to provide, he had me sit before untouched meals long into the night. I had the advantages of being anemic and of having a mother who cried at my refusal to eat. After three weeks he gave in. I ate at her nightstand instead. Until my divorce, this instance would remain the one time I disobeyed him.

But as soon as he visited each new maid, I began to imitate her gestures, voice, and walk; sometimes, staring at his back, I felt my heart knock loudly in my throat.

I am ten, my mother and I are on our way back from the grocery store, shopping with her is still a treat for me, she has only recently been well enough to leave the house. She interrupts a recital of what she would like to buy at the butcher if given a choice, and what we would, in fact, be able to afford, to say under her breath, between a whisper and a hiss, "Across the street. Don't stare. She's the latest one."

It is a young woman with black hair. She wears fragile high heels on a winter afternoon, there are mud flecks on slender, stockinged ankles, the curve of white cheek nestled in fur. No hat, snowflakes on glossy black.

Never before have my mother and I exchanged so much as a glance, acknowledging to one another what both of us knew. Now I pretend not to have heard her.

"The latest" was the last. My father found a job in a factory, joined a handful of laborers who "got together after work, pretending to be a brass band," multiplied the number of musicians, started a second group, and ended up with a large and raucously cheerful band as well as an orchestra of respectable size before buying his plot of land. Then he put conducting aside, too.

"*Meine grosse Liebe*," she tells me—my great love. I am in Austria on a visit, married, two children. "Now, now, *Mutti*," I say and smile and think, *Schmalz*, the stuff of magazine stories for women of her time. But she repeats, "He was my great love, and he is, and he will always be my great love."

The last part of her sentence silenced me, even then, at a time when I still saw myself as happily married. Now I think, To say that and to mean it is a statement of sweep; who among my friends would speak in such terms about a husband, a wife, a lover?

"We've been lucky until now." "Let's hope for the best." "Knock on wood." "So far, so good." My friends and I substitute one of these cautious formulas for the last item on my mother's trinity, we stay away from theological language, absolutist language, conviction, faith.

"Come on," I said back then. "Think about who you're talking to. I was around, remember? Don't tell me it was all roses, you must have hated him, too. Didn't you? Never? Just temporarily? After all, if even I knew about his . . . women."

"You don't know," she said, and then, "What do *you* know?"

"I wasn't blind," I said. "And my hearing was fine, too."

"You don't know how he cared for me during—"

"Oh, you're wrong," I said. "I do know all that, washing you and whatever, but what does that have to do with it?"

"You know so little," she said. "And all the wrong things. I urinated into a mason jar, and he held it against the light, morning and night, nearly three years. He saved my life more than once. He got so good at it, he came to know two days in advance when things were turning bad again, he'd run to the doctor with the jar in a paper bag, holding it as if it were his own blood. Just because of a different shade, a change of smell. It meant nothing to me or a doctor—they needed lab tests first—but he could tell. The doctors were amazed by him, they told me so. Whenever I had to go back to the hospital it was only for a few days, he always caught a flare-up of the infection before it got to be a disaster. Washing your wife is one thing, and even that gets to be a dreary business. But what man do you know who checks his sick wife's urine every day?"

She waited for an answer. "His women—" My mother, who gestured rarely, lifted her right forearm into the air, the sleeve of her housedress fell back, she bent her wrist just barely, as if she meant to wave aside a small fly. "He stood by me and took care of me, a tedious and unappetizing sickness, not picturesque like a case of consumption or pneumonia, over in three weeks or months. Would your husband do it for you?"

She waited again. "Besides, all you know about his affairs is that they happened. All you know is the obvious. There is more to people than that."

I detested and adored my father while he was alive and I still do, I feared, admired, envied and loved him and I still do, though the maggots must surely be done with him by now. I miss and only miss my mother.

I'm in the bomb shelter, my mother has disappeared, a woman I do not know holds my hand, she speaks in a cheerful voice, ". . . strewed bread crumbs, wasn't that clever?" But I already know that birds will eat the crumbs. I should also know that Hänsel and Gretel live happily ever after, but now I cannot remember how the story ends. I only know that they are lost, alone in the woods, in the dark, *Mutti, Mutti, Mutti.* . . . . "You just can't see her right now, because of the crowd," says the woman at my side. "Listen to the story, you'll never guess what happens next." But the stranger's kindness only warms my hand.

"She never talked about herself" is true. Also true is that I asked no questions. I was consumed with myself—fourteen, fifteen, sixteen—after all, she had grown up in the sticks, how could she understand what my friends and I thought important, what did she know?

Once I blurted out to her, "James Dean is the greatest actor in the world." She looked up from her knitting machine and said, "When I was young, two different people told me that I looked like Ingrid Bergman . . . a little." Then she finished the interrupted row.

At least she was spared the expression on my face. I looked at her thickening neck—it was mottled; she was blushing—at her heavy body in its housedress and apron, at her gray hair tucked out of the way with no design in mind, a bobby pin about to come loose. *Ingrid Berman*, I thought, *how deluded can one poor woman get?*

Another time I decided to treat her to a rousing synopsis of the movie just then holding my friends and me in thrall. I had barely sketched a few scenes when she said, "I think I am getting confused." A little while later she smiled. "You really like this movie, don't you?" I nodded, impatient and annoyed, and went on. Before I was halfway through she said, "What a complicated story."

I said, "I'll do my homework at Ilse's house," and left.

Most of our discussions of this movie took place during religious education class. Our professor taught *Gymnasium* pupils during the day and courses at the university at night; half an hour into a class, and continuing to sit straight-necked behind his desk, he would close his eyes. Though we knew that to raise our voices above a whisper was a waste of precious time—he would blink his puffy lids then and read a parable out loud before resuming his nap—this particular discussion awoke our priest for weeks. One group insisted that its hero was sensitively handsome, truly romantic, a poet of the heart; the others would hiss, "But he's such a creep! God, all I ever want out of life is Rhett!"

Twenty years later, watching the very same Rhett on television in New York, I keep thinking how much rather I'd listen to Mammy scold Scarlett in German.

I decide to "do my face." It is a break in my routine, no more, no less, since once again no one will see me except the doorman, when I go downstairs to get the mail. I wash my face with a special, overpriced soap, after oiling it with a special, overpriced oil. *Fourteen, fifteen, maybe she watched children.* I spread a special, overpriced cream on my oiled and washed face, then remove the cream with a liquid that, by the looks of it, might be water. *Always liked school, but she hired herself out as a Saudirn.* I put rouge on my cheeks, I push my hair off my forehead, she used to do that, it was the closest she came to caressing me.

This is how genes work, at their simplest and most predictable: my father had black hair, my mother was blond, here I am, mine's brown. Except that my brother inherited my mother's coloring undiluted by my father's, and he devotes his life to music.

"Not guitar," my father said to him, early on. "Any instruments you want, just not guitar." But Ernsti was unlike me and undaunted by my father. Much later, he ran off to London with a female colleague, another musician. He was married by then and lived upstairs in my parents' house with his wife and two children. After a few weeks he came back. My father stood in the doorway, greeting him with the words, "You will not enter my house again." I would have turned on my heel. But my brother said, "What are you talking about? I *live* here," and walked past my father through the door and down the hallway.

To me, the astonished onlooker, Ernest-Werner Seiler had always seemed able to bypass our father. As a boy he practiced the violin at home but plucked on a friend's guitar, in friends' basements, for hours, for months. He learned to play the guitar as my father had learned to play French horn and tuba and whatever else, on borrowed instruments. Eventually he swapped something —bicycle parts?—for a guitar of his own, practicing often and never at home. When he had taught himself what he considered enough for the purpose, he began to give lessons, charging money to be spent on a better guitar, then a better one yet. Failing one subject in school this year, a different one the year after, yet another *Gymnasium* throwing him out, the reason always the same: "insubordination."

At nineteen he took a teaching job in a country school. I have a photograph of him posing with his class, he looks sixteen, there are nearly forty children. Smiling country girls wearing *Dirndl* outfits or aprons over their round-collared blouses, a few of the boys mug for the camera. He stuck it out for a couple of years, then went on the road with a band, singing American rock lyrics, playing Beatle songs on the guitar, good money. In off hours he practiced sixteenth-century rondos, flamenco. Later yet he began, on weekdays, to amass the courses and exams that would allow him to teach music at a university, financing his studies through weekend rock band excursions—"Groupies, it was fun."

Now, in addition to teaching music full-time, he is working toward the exams that will make him a conductor. Officially, that is; he's had years of unofficial experience conducting various student orchestras. Being able to play the piano is, so he explains to me, one of the skills required of a conductor, and he fears the piano exam. My father (who regretted that he had never mastered the piano himself) was furious at my brother's refusal to play the piano, but he could only pressure his daughter into taking lessons on this particular instrument. At the time, the official violin and the secret guitar were enough for my brother, the piano seemed useless. "It's hard," he says now. "I started in my late twenties, there's no catching up on a piano, the others started as kids, it's a shame. . . ."

Still, my brother has inherited and taken on the best in his father, along with the light hair, the flexibility, the cliché "Austrian" temperament of our mother. He is an easygoing man who enjoys a hearty meal with a gusto foreign to me, he is choosy about wines, he drinks good brandy in small amounts, he shuns affiliation with political parties, he is happy in Austria and intends to stay there. A handsome, big man who takes just the right pause before the punch line in the jokes he loves to tell and who exuberantly fingers the dashboard of his new car, aglitter with knobs, "What a toy, what a gorgeous toy."

My brother's passions, though they sometimes conflict, are well defined: music, his family, comfort, Austria. The larger half of his inheritance was spent on the apartment in which he and his family now live, but part of it immediately went into a plot of land, not large but very pretty. Half an hour's driving distance from Graz, it slopes down a hill, improbably and overwhelmingly giving the illusion of undiscovered territory, bright with wild flowers among high grass.

My share has gone to pay off debts—no small matter that. It had come to a point where I could no longer manage, here in New York. My brother pleaded with me to come home, an untenable solution for me. So he sold the house. It grieved him, though he denied it to me at the time and still does. What was left after the debts were paid went into wallpaper for my room, having a flaking bathroom painted glossy white. There is a sum put away for my daughter; by the time she will need it for college tuition it may not cover a semester's worth of study. And for a few months there was a high three-figure amount in my checking account—luxury.

That's where it went, Seiler's Bunker, the house he built brick by brick. That's where it went after the fixtures and plumbing of the second kitchen had been torn out, an extra kitchen being an impediment to a sale, an additional bedroom representing yet one more plus. While he put all those thousands and thousands of bricks onto wet mortar, did my father see us there, the two of us—the two of them dead as they are now—my brother and me, one of us living downstairs using the downstairs kitchen, the other one a flight above, using the second one? A fortress to cement his family together, intended for our protection, impenetrable; grandchildren under the apple trees he planted, safe behind a high fence, a locked gate? Now his son lives in a comfortable apartment on the other side of town, though he devotes his life to music as his father might have wished to do, and he does own a plot of land, which might be of consolation to both his parents. The other one is a stranger to Austria, has no creditors for the time being, and rents a room in New York. The fortress came to little in the end.

I put a dusting of overpriced powder on my forehead and nose, *always liked school*, eyebrow pencil, lipstick. She was alone in Vienna at fourteen, and he rolled off a set of tracks and ran. But the army liked him for his versatility as a musician, and one of his children, at least, has stepped into those footsteps, though his daughter is unable to pick out a tune on the piano he made her take lessons on for three years. I hum along with the radio, by myself, and I loved singing nursery songs to my children, they did not care how far off pitch I was. My claim on music is a worn satchel filled with fragments. *Eine kleine Nachtmusik,* the shiny star of the lot, nudges up against "I can't get no, I can't get no . . ." The schlockiest parts of *Die Fledermaus* jostle Beethoven's *Für Elise,* Ella Fitzgerald and Louis Armstrong crooning "A foggy day . . ." and "Stars fell on Alabama . . . ," a little David Bowie, Randy Newman. (The relief of walking out of Lincoln Center in the middle of the first act of a Wagner thing, to the dismay of a friend who had reserved our tickets months in advance and then would not stop telling me how gloriously the Rhine swamps the stage in the third act.) A pop song lilts at the bottom. My mother sang it in the forties and long into the fifties, when it had not been on the radio for more than a decade.

> *Es geht alles vorüber, es geht alles vorbei,*
> *Auf jeden Dezember folgt wieder ein Mai . . .*

something like, "Everything passes, everything comes to an end, each December is followed by another May." Soldiers listened to it on field radios and hummed it, dug first into frozen mud, then deeply into snow, before Stalingrad. Women sang it on assembly lines in munitions factories and while concocting birthday cakes for their children according to newspaper recipes telling them how to shape mashed potatoes into icing. That song, equally banal in lyrics and melody, comforts me, as does my mother's most Carinthian of folksongs, its lyrics improbable as balm, "Forsaken, forsaken, I'm as forsaken as a pebble in the middle of the road." But the words mean as little as those of that other song, "Raise high the flags." And the first few bars of my father's favorite march, played by the Americans in 1955, at the ceremony dreamed up by the four occupiers, when they were ready to leave us after all. The three other military bands had played their own anthems, but the Americans had played the "Star-Spangled Banner" and then Strauss's "Radetzky March," "a nice touch," the newspapers called it. The bottom of my satchel is reserved for the waltz whose Austrian name proved too long for an impatient translator, its full name, as given by its composer, being *"An der schönen, blauen Donau."*

What will I wear, is my first thought. Andy has invited me to his Bar Mitzvah. Two days before the event I call his mother. She tells me she has bought a special dress, but that anything short of jeans will do for me.

Though the synagogue is only a block away, I leave fifteen minutes early, get there in three, and am late after all. Something is clearly in progress. A man at the far end of a long room is chanting, Andy and his family are sitting up front, a few other people are sprinkled here and there. Confused, I tiptoe to a chair in the middle of the last row.

As soon as I am seated, an elderly man who has been standing near the doorway walks down my row, nods, smiles, and hands me an open book. I nod and smile in return and bend my head over the pages. But while the text is printed in both Hebrew and English, the chanting is only in Hebrew. I read the English passages and turn to a different page as soon as its number is announced. I am clumsy at finding a new section, and, maddeningly, not just the first time around. The page numbers run backward. Soon I would rather look around. I lay the book on my lap and let the next page change go by. At once, a different gray-haired man makes his way down my row and finds my page for me. Flustered, a first-grader caught daydreaming, I manage to hold the book open at the correct place, stealthily looking up between page calls. Andy is wearing a black-and-gold yarmulke.

More people file in, now there are a few in almost every row. The rows consist of metal chairs upholstered in red vinyl, the carpet running down the center aisle is equally red, the walls are bare. The man up front continues to sing. I am unable to pick out a melody or progression. It is a foreign fantasy tune, reminiscent of what my children sometimes sang themselves to sleep with, forlorn cadences going nowhere.

I settle deeper into my chair which is, vinyl or not, more comfortable than a wooden pew. The behavior of this congregation is mysterious to someone used to a body of worshipers moving, in fact, as one body. (Before our wedding, the groom had reassured a nervous, and Baptist, matron of honor that she would have no difficulties at all; she should simply imitate the best man at her side. When her neighbor's left leg happened to go to sleep during a long period of kneeling, the matron of honor had reproduced each of his attempts at arising, each little thump back down, the grasping of a knee in both hands, the massaging of a calf, each surreptitious shake of a leg. They had been at the altar rail up front, in full view of a congregation marveling in silence.)

This group has no truck with uniform responses. Are

individual people intoning the same text as the cantor, but trailing him by a couple of words so that the overlap makes it sound as if they are chanting a different passage? Or *are* they chanting a different passage? Or are they really reciting elaborate rejoinders? There is an informality about this intoning, a randomness, none of the orderly alternation of priest–people, priest–priest, and people–priest. A man who has been standing and chanting emphatically sits down, crosses his legs, closes his book. A second one stands, reading silently. A seated woman now and then says a few words to herself in a low voice. Amazing, I think, Christians behave like sheep in comparison. Well, that *is* what we're supposed to be, "The Lord is my . . ." What these worshipers seem to be doing, as observed by an uninitiate, is improvising rituals on the spot; it strikes me as inviting, at least in principle, though this whole thing does go on a bit, what has it been now, an hour?

But now Andy is standing up front, he begins his chant. I know this boy's voice well, and what it sounds like in a range of moods, but I have not heard this voice before. It is far stronger than I have expected, deeper than usual, utterly self-assured. He's great, I think, *the kid's great*, and after all his fretting, "The easy part's in big print, would you believe it, and the hard part's in little print. . . ." There is a tap on my shoulder. A round-faced, middle-aged woman says, and not in a whisper at all, "I wish somebody'd push his hair out of his eyes, don't you?" Just then, a man in the row ahead of me picks up his book, leafs through it noisily, and begins to read out loud, lagging a syllable or so behind Andy, producing an infuriating, rumbling echo. Some nerve, I think, as a second man begins to intone as well and a third. All this time they've refused to do anything in unison; now that it's his big moment they feel compelled to join in? But Andy does not seem to hear them. He neither wavers nor stumbles once, no wonder he was nervous, I think, this thing is endless.

His speech comes next.

"I thank this congregation for being here. I am glad to be Bar Mitzvahed. I am happy to be a Jew. Thank you."

This is the greatest speech I've ever heard, I think, and deeply bend my head, for some minutes unable to suppress my smile.

Half a dozen sentences into the rabbi's sermon I am impressed and touched. It is a sermon tailor-made for Andy. Sci-fi stuff, astronauts, lunar visions, the triumphs of technology, Sarah the center of a moon cult, Abraham embracing monotheism, astronauts again, Andy is leaning forward in his chair. Conscious, suddenly, of feeling not a shred of animosity within me, I try to dredge some up. No success. I quickly squelch my surprise. You're on a field trip here, remember? This is not real life. A pleasant exercise in "contrast and compare," complete with the dilettante anthropologist's edge of benign superiority, aren't the natives' customs quaint? The sermon is longer than Andy's chant. I crave a cigarette.

Now there is something like a hymn after all, sung loudly and communally. For the first time since the beginning of this service I am aware of the absence of organ music. Fine, I think, a sign of good taste, it's a toss-up between organs and bagpipes for most obnoxious instrument. But incense, come to think of it, I could do with some of that, the sweep of a censer on thin, gold chains, gray-blue smoke blurring the altar, making you squint, filling your nostrils with its heavy, voluptuous smell. All at once I am weary of sitting in such a brightly lit room, no shadowy recesses anywhere, no dark, wooden confessionals, nooks for competing saints painted in faded colors and gilt, the opulent gleam of brocade and gold chalices, dust particles afloat in muted shafts of light tinted by stained glass, convoluted crossbeams of stone way up high; lighting a votive candle on tiptoes, "Holy Mary, please, if you . . . I'll never talk back to my mother again."

But there is a surprise at the end. A procession forms down the aisle behind a man carrying the Torah, as intricate and shiny and decorative as the monstrance carried by the priest, he walks under an embroidered canopy, little girls run ahead to throw floppy peony petals in his path, each of us had a basketful and we hoarded them, the procession was a lot less fun once you'd run out of petals; kneeling at the side of the road in last year's First Communion dress with the hem let out; the night before, my mother would moisten my hair with sugar water and braid it tightly while fireworks rumbled on the hills behind Graz, dreadful Good Friday was over and that limbo of a Saturday too, Easter tomorrow; it would hang to my waist in a cloud, sticky and popular with flies, licentious, the only day of the year when I'm allowed outside with my hair hanging loose, I feel it float behind me as I run.

The reception is next. "I hope you don't mind," Andy has said, apologetically but firmly. "You're only invited to that, the lunch is just sort of for the family."

The small, upstairs room is filled with smiling and chattering people. I spot a chair between the end of a long table and the wall, with a wall behind it. Perfect, I think. But though this method of making myself unapproachable has served me well at many parties, it does not work here. A white-haired man smiles at me broadly and offers me a glass of wine, an elderly woman hands me a plate with something whitish on it. "Gefilte fish," she says as I wince inside. Her smile is as warm as her predecessor's. What a speech, she says, and didn't he do well with his Hebrew? Such a lovely boy! She used to teach, Andy's father had been one of her pupils, why aren't you eating? she says, eat! I gobble the dreadful stuff as if it were vanilla pudding. Across the room, Andy seems in the grip of a powerful drug. It gives a reckless shine to his eyes and robs him of all expressions but a dazed smile.

When I notice that the rabbi is putting on his coat I introduce myself and tell him how thoughtful I find it that he had taken the pains to preach an hour-long sermon so uniquely appropriate for Andy. "Oh, really?" he says, tucking a scarf around his throat. "I wasn't aware of that, I don't really know him very well." In an effort not to laugh out loud, I watch him rumble down the stairs. When I find Andy's mother to thank her, she says, "Oh, well, we really would like you to come to lunch, a restaurant near here, do come."

The adults sit at a long table, Andy and his friends at a small one. How nice, I think, he has a separate party, but why is he made to sit at a kiddie table today, of all days? ("Becoming a man, I ask you, what is that supposed to mean? Right then? Right there? How can I be a boy one day and a man the next?") I do not ask either Andy's father to my right or his former teacher to my left about the philosophy behind the seating arrangements, I ask no questions at all, I am determined to blend in as best I can. This is not just another lunch celebrating someone's birthday or raise. Most of the Jews I know are my age and single, I see them at work or at parties or over small dinners. I have never been at a gathering as intimate as this one, young Jews and old ones, family and friends.

Drinks are ordered, more drinks, appetizers, soup, wine, we're on our way. The party has been animated from the start and soon turns very lively. Joke follows joke, now there seem to be several in progress at once. Clusters of people burst into laughter in short succession, the bantering on one end of the table blooms into heated argument as diners join in one by one, the level of excitement in the voices around me spells impending melee. Yet throughout, there is a curious lack of edge to it all. These noisy exchanges herald neither fistfights nor broken friendships. I have no memories of such a gathering, none. Instead, I carry with me a string-wrapped parcel of longing for just such a table, just such raucousness and ease. The mute meals at my grandparents' farm, physical exhaustion as palpable as food, the adults around me battered into silence as if by Thorazine; a plate on my mother's nightstand; wordless meals later, my brother (fresh from another thrashing by his father) aloof as if dining on Mars; my first lunch with a classmate, a uniformed maid waiting on two eleven-year-

237

olds, a room just to eat in and a cloth napkin for the first time, my equal at school a remote princess now, formidable . . .*This* is what I've missed? A table of Jews annoying other restaurant patrons with their exuberance? They give us sidelong glances, one man catches my eye and frowns, I wink at him and grin, he turns his back. One voice booms above all others. A large man from the other end of the table has begun to squeeze his bulk in my direction, balancing his heaped plate and silverware above his head, roaring, "Ingeborg, my wife wants us to trade seats, she loves writers and wants to talk to yoooo-hoooo!"

Fake an upset stomach, a leg cramp, a forgotten appointment, too late. I pick up my plate, murmur "Excuse me" to my neighbors, and find myself ensconced between Andy's mother and the woman who loves writers. She has a florid face and wears a low-cut blouse dripping with lace. "My husband is right," her voice is as resonant as his. "I do love writers. Now tell me all about it, *what kind of book are you writing?*"

Panic manipulates my vocal cords. "It's, I'm, uh . . . it's an erotic epic poem."

I want to kiss everyone around me. They've burst out laughing, a man proposes a toast, the woman across from me raises her eyebrows and repeats my words, slowly drawing out each syllable, there is a new round of laughter, someone begins to tell a joke, a toast now to the Bar Mitzvah boy. But Andy has been sitting on a banquette, the table before him is heavy, the boys across from him have wedged their captain's chairs against it, he cannot straighten his knees. "Get up, Andy," says his father and, more loudly, *"Get up!"* Andy, in a half crouch that gives him no leverage, pushes against the table. His face turns red. I stand still and upright, glass in hand. *"Come on,"* shouts his father, *"damn it, straighten your knees, son, stand up!"* The boy lets his hair fall over his eyes. Two men finally move the table. "A toast to my son on this great occasion, to my wonderful son."

When we sit down, the mood has changed. Until I leave, the

first guest to do so and taking with me an extra piece of Andy's mother's cake, I listen in silence to stories about relatives fleeing Poland.

Toward late afternoon Andy calls. "Can I come up? My parents are taking a nap." He brings along a stocky, slow-spoken friend, the two boys are each other's perfect foils. Andy talks incessantly and at great speed, swiveling in my typing chair until he has to hold his head in his hands. The comparative merits of teachers, does God exist? a brief excursion on the topic of hookers, life after death, science fiction, he is in extraordinary form. "How can you believe that Jesus came back to life?" he asks his friend, who frowns but does not answer. "Do you really believe that? Really, truly?" "Yeah," says the friend. "But how *can* you?" says Andy, and launches into a series of concisely presented logical arguments against such an occurrence, a body's tendency to decompose figuring as leitmotiv. I do my best to keep my expression bland. The stocky boy has refused to take off his heavily padded parka and eyes me sideways from under heavy lids. No counterargument is forthcoming. Andy pushes. "Come on," he says, "say something, come on, what do you say?" The other boy looks up and says, carefully enunciating each word, "Get off my back." "But why?" insists Andy, he is flying high, if he has not become a man today he might temporarily be an angel disguised as a slender boy on speed, adrenaline has set him afloat, a beatific speed freak smiling a beatific smile, swiveling maniacally, his insinuating voice at odds with a rapid-fire delivery, "Just tell me why. . . ." "The Church says so," growls the stocky boy. "My mother says so, get off my back." "Oh," says Andy, and, "Well," and, "Even so, that doesn't mean we can't talk about it, does it?" But his friend is sullen now and a few minutes later he has to go home.

Any other time I would have sent Andy on the errand I need done before the neighborhood stores close, but somehow that doesn't seem appropriate today. Since he does not appear ready to leave, I ask him to come along with me. The errand is accomplished in a few minutes. We stand on a sloshy sidewalk, our hands in our pockets, I thank him again for his invitation. Does he want to go someplace and have dinner? No, he says, he's been eating all day. A soda then? Yes, he'll have a soda. Our table is slick with grease, the floor littered and sticky. You could have bought him a glass of wine somewhere, I think, what a paltry way to end the day, sitting in a miserable Burger King. He tells me about his latest finds, gleaned during hours spent in secondhand record stores. "You have to read the titles on the spines, sideways, that's how they're lined up on the shelves, it gives you a pain in the neck." He often buys a record for the sound of a group's name, Arkansas . . . Lonely . . .

My daughter, Ursula, and I are spending Christmas in Graz. There is the tree, bare, having been brought into the apartment on the morning of Christmas Eve. It is being decorated by my sister-in-law and her two children and my remaining one. There are the candles ("What? Fire hazard? Who ever heard of a Christmas tree catching afire . . ."), there is tinsel, there are intricate homemade ornaments of woven straw. Toward evening my brother's parents-in-law arrive with their son. My brother lights the candles. My niece, who has my mother's and my son's light hair, recites a poem, shy and exuberant at once. My nephew, who has my color hair and my son's mouth and chin, plays a violin so tiny it seems made for a doll. My brother smiles at his son steadily and encouragingly, and when he winces, only once and with amusement, the boy does not notice. My niece plays a Christmas carol on the piano and her mother accompanies her on the flute. Finally, my brother plays the guitar as we all sing *"Stille Nacht."* Here this song is sung only once a year, on Christmas Eve, it is not just any carol; a village schoolmaster and the organist of the local church had concocted that song in December 1818, when the organ in their snowed-in Austrian mountain village had broken down and they'd been determined to have special music for Christmas, after all. I think, but do not say, that a continent away, beginning the day after Thanksgiving, this song repeats itself every hour on the hour, an integral part of Holiday Season Muzak in New York City's office-building elevators.

We open our presents then, and while the children finger their new toys amid capitalist-size heaps of wrapping paper the adults drink a *Bowle* made by my sister-in-law. "You start it in the spring," she says, "and you add whatever fruits you like, as they come into season, apricots, berries." The brew slides down easy as the most harmless of wines, deceptive and potent.

My daughter is entranced, it is her first Austrian Christmas. So am I, it is my first as an adult.

On New Year's Eve we celebrate early. Ursula and I need to return to our hotel, our plane is scheduled for nine in the morning, our train to Vienna leaves Graz at six a.m. The first snow of the winter has started to come down in midafternoon. By late evening (Ursula packs methodically, occasionally throwing a disapproving glance at my more haphazard methods but refraining from comment) the snow has become the snow of my childhood. Fat flakes descend in a profusion so dense that looking at it coming down, trying to focus on it, makes your head spin.

Toward midnight I order a small bottle of champagne. The

room-service clerk is flushed and amiable, I tip him recklessly. We open the window wide, its two tall wings fold back into the room. We wrap a down comforter around us and lean out into the snow, a few flakes melt into our champagne. To our right we can see a portion of the Main Square and half of my *Rathaus*, no flags. The bells start to ring, every church bell in Graz rings, it's midnight. Windows all around us are flung open, parties are at their height behind each of the glowing squares, revelers shout New Year's greetings to strangers leaning out of windows across the street, down the block, to us; firecrackers pop and dazzle, the bells clamor on.

In front of the *Rathaus*—we just miss seeing it but we can hear it clearly—a band begins to play. At a streetcar stop nearby, a group of people huddles in the snow. We watch two figures glide off the sidewalk and onto the streetcar tracks, they put their arms around each other and begin to waltz. The group dissolves as if on stage, on cue, it's all couples now in heavy boots and coats and hats, waltzing. The bells ring, the invisible band plays, the small, bundled-up figures twirl as if weightless in the deserted street. When the streetcar comes along its driver stops his engine a distance down the tracks, he waits while the waltz rouses and spins to its end. Ursula, her champagne gone and possibly gone to her dear, half-Austrian head, leans far over the edge of the windowsill, checking the sidewalk below. Then she smiles at me and winks and throws up her arm, the sleeve of her nightgown falls back from her round and smooth little elbow, as smooth and round as only my mother's has ever been. She flings the empty glass up and out into the air. By now there is too much snow on the ground for us to hear it land.